AS THE ROMANS DO

La Dolce Vita in a Cookbook
Classic and Reinvented Recipes from Rome

ELEONORA GALASSO

Photography by David Loftus

To Nonna Ia, always protecting me from above the stars

An Hachette UK Company
www.hachette.co.uk

First published in Great Britain in 2016 by
Mitchell Beazley, a division of Octopus Publishing Group Ltd
Carmelite House
50 Victoria Embankment
London EC4Y 0DZ
www.octopusbooks.co.uk
www. octopusbooksusa.com

Distributed in the US by
Hachette Book Group
1290 Avenue of the Americas
4th and 5th Floors
New York, NY 10020

Distributed in Canada by
Canadian Manda Group
664 Annette St.
Toronto, Ontario, Canada M6S 2C8

ISBN 978 1 78472 160 2

A CIP catalog record for this book is available from
the British Library.

Printed and bound in China

10 9 8 7 6 5 4 3 2 1

Senior Commissioning Editor: Eleanor Maxfield
Art Director: Juliette Norsworthy
Senior Editor: Alex Stetter
Copy Editors: Simon Davis, Constance Novis
Photographer: David Loftus (except pp 8, 11, 65 top right and
153 bottom left: Cecilia Fusco; p 302 top row center: Olivia Magris)
Home Economists and Food Stylists: Emily Ezekiel, Sian Henley
Props Stylist: Linda Berlin
Illustrator: Grace Helmer
Assistant Production Manager: Caroline Alberti

AS THE ROMANS DO

La Dolce Vita in a Cookbook
Classic and Reinvented Recipes from Rome

ELEONORA GALASSO

Photography by David Loftus

MITCHELL BEAZLEY

CONTENTS

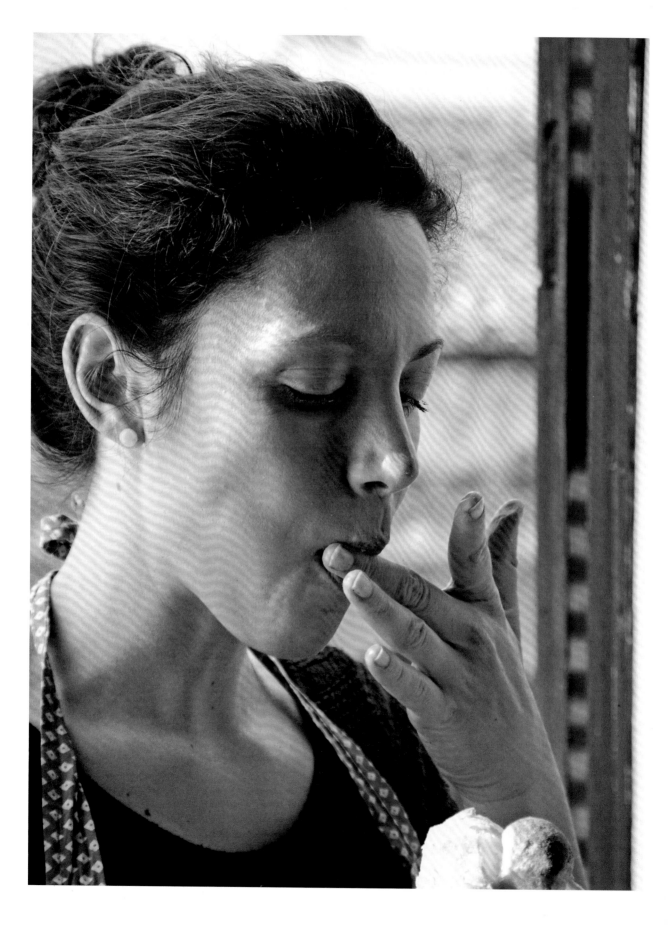

INTRODUCTION

Food is a language and just like any other language, it needs to be decoded. I'm a Food Interpreter. Follow me and you will discover the secrets of the Roman table in all its wonderfully complex simplicity.

This book is for anyone who has ever wanted to make Italian food but was unsure where to start; it is also for anyone who thinks that Italian food is mostly about the joys of pasta and pizza. This book is for those unafraid to enter a new, hidden dimension of Italian gastronomic delights, from treats for early risers to dishes for midnight feasts, as well as revamped versions of classic recipes. My food is full of flavor and perfect for all home kitchens around the world. The recipes reflect authentic Italian home cooking, which requires no special ingredients or unusual equipment. Some recipes I inherited from my family, passed down from generation to generation, others I collected traveling around the Lazio region, accumulating secrets and techniques from an eclectic cast of characters for whom eating "the Italian way" is not a lifestyle statement but a necessity.

The style of casual entertaining that can be found in households all over the world is simply magnified in Italy. I believe this is the reason behind the international love for Italian cuisine: it brings togetherness to a natural peak. Quality time spent with friends and family when time and space disappear to give way to good conversation, with everyone cooking together in the hustle and bustle of a kitchen that, no matter how big or how small, is always the heart of a home. Finally the words "*È pronto a tavola!*" are uttered, and when the meal is over there's a gratifying sense of contentment and of time well spent.

I divide my time between Rome, Paris, and London, yet—much as I love traveling—there's not a corner on earth where I've seen the entire world pass by more than sitting at my own table. To me, it's a place from which to put the world to rights through sweet chats, sparkly exchanges, or feisty debates that offers, above all, an uncontaminated, deep sense of participation. Each person is entitled to their own vision and each course has a story to tell: food is the key to unlocking life. My idea of the perfect meal is about achieving that sense of unconditional belonging, the search for which lets us all wander from land to land and, once that sense of "home" is finally found, allows us to sit down and say: "Hey, I quite like it here. I think I'm going to stay for a while."

My recipes are down-to-earth and speak to the heart; easy on the wallet, unfussy meals for singles, couples, friends, and families. You can play with the methods and adapt them to a variety of circumstances: quick and earthy breakfasts, vivacious *al fresco* meals, brilliant off-the-cuff dinner parties. It's all about finding your own food happiness, even if it's just an espresso and a spoonful of ricotta and honey—enjoy it with a grin on your face and a feeling of kitchen satisfaction as life takes on a different pace.

Rome is a layered city, the result of centuries of splendid and impressive urban chaos. It is bruised and magnified by all its eras, each of which has left its mark and an artful array of enveloping buildings and stirring personalities. There is classical Rome, the medieval city, the Renaissance, the Baroque, the Rome after 1870, when the city became the capital of the Kingdom of Italy. Then there is the Rome of *La Dolce Vita*—the cafés, the indomitably cheerful characters, the Vespas, the whistling at girls, the long walks in open-air museums, and that inexplicable and enchanting confusion that takes possession of every visitor, leaving them spellbound.

I like to call myself a crusader of good food and eating well. *As The Romans Do* pays tribute to the mysteries behind the gastronomic culture of Rome and its surroundings—you'll feel like you're walking with me through the Roman breeze. I'll take you on a journey through the tiny side streets, the grand palazzos, the traditions, the communities, and the hidden gems of this eternal city to discover what "Romanity" is truly about. In Rome, the aroma of a strong coffee will wake me up, the fragrance of thin, oily *pizza bianca* will guide me through the morning, and an indescribable mixture of burnt wood and tomato sauce will remind me that it's time for lunch. You don't need a watch in a city where time is marked by the smells drifting from kitchens and the ringing of church bells. When exploring the Roman way of life, keep your eyes, nose, and ears wide open.

With this book, I set out to share atmospheres and fragrances that are familiar to me and that I hope will become just as familiar to you as you flip through the pages of this account of sweet idleness, or *dolce far niente*, as we say in Italy. Here is my quintessential *captatio benevolentiæ*: Cook, Eat, and Talk. The Roman Way.

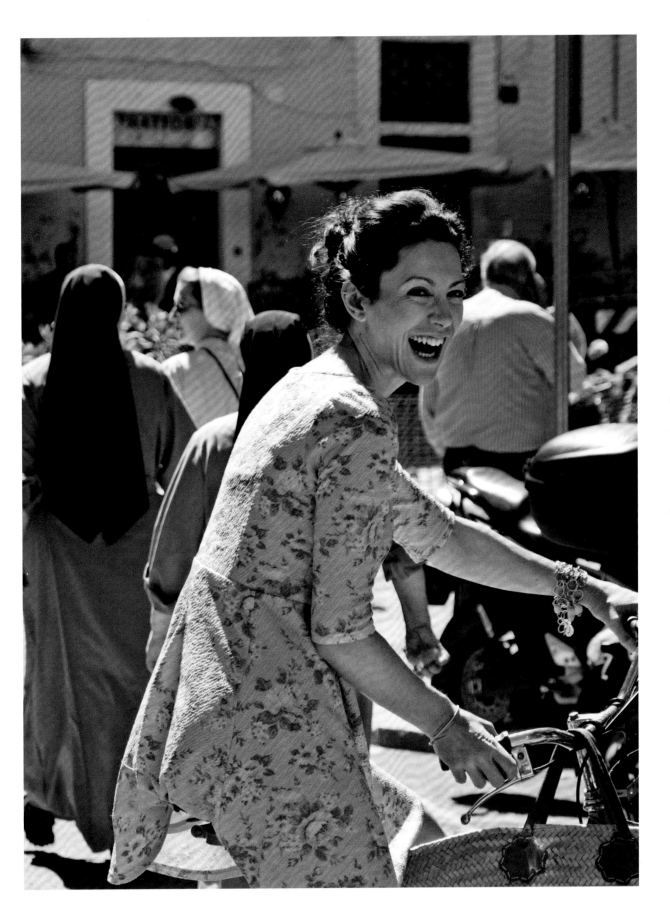

THE ROMAN CUPBOARD

There are some staples you will find in every Roman kitchen. Having the following items on hand will help you cook The Roman Way—these ingredients are the *sine qua non* for Roman epicurean living and becoming a food gladiator:

• When Romans say olive oil, we mean "extra virgin cold-pressed olive oil." The oil is extracted by pressing the olives without adding heat, thereby retaining their full nutritional value and aroma. Any dish will gain an unmistakable kick from this luminous golden condiment.

• Romans always keep a cooking wine or *vino da cucina* handy, which is a cheap, full-flavored wine from the local countryside. Not only is a good red wine stain on the tablecloth synonymous with a happy meal, we also use wine in many recipes, from stews to savory pies.

• It goes without saying that eggs should be freerange if possible, but it's fundamental they are extra fresh and at room temperature.

• Romans love herbs—their perfume is so intoxicating—but we are not prescriptive about their use. You can't go wrong by adding basil, parsley, rosemary, thyme, sage, or any fresh herb, you name it, to most dishes.

• Pasta is a fundamental component of any Italian pantry. We're not snobs about shapes and brands, but for special occasions, we'll treat ourselves. Pricier pasta is likely to have been made using the bronze wire-drawing method, which makes its surface rougher and allows it to hold sauces well. And once you've learned how to make your own pasta, you'll be able to produce as many variations on the theme as you wish.

• Use either carnaroli or arborio rice to ensure impeccable results for dishes from *timballi* to fried *supplì* (*see* pages 184 and 134).

• All Romans have a natural affinity for anchovies, perhaps because they featured as the main ingredient in *garum*, a sun-dried fermented fish sauce in vogue in Ancient Rome. Anchovies are perfect in salads, or as part of a luscious filling for fresh egg pasta.

• In many Roman households, a big batch of stock is prepared ahead of the coming culinary week. To make vegetable stock, half-fill a large saucepan with water, chuck in a peeled carrot, a celery stalk, a tomato, a potato, and a large peeled white onion studded with a few cloves, and cook everything for 20 minutes. It's that simple.

• *Soffritto* is a translucent combination of very finely chopped carrot, garlic, onion, and celery that, added to a pan with some olive oil and allowed to sweat down for a few minutes, will transform the base of every sauce and condiment, whether vegetable-, fish-, or meat-based.

• Ricotta (especially the kind made from sheep milk) is something you buy as regularly in Rome as bread and onions. Use it on top of your salads or add it to your pasta. Its flavor is so mild it goes well with everything, from meat and fish dishes to cake or your breakfast toast.

• Romans keep jars and jars of tomato sauce in the pantry, even if that means sacrificing a good bottle of wine. I've included a foolproof recipe for making your own whenever you feel like it (*see* page 254).

• The butter Romans use is unsalted. You won't see it used often in this book because butter is more characteristic of the food of northern Italy, whereas from Tuscany down most recipes call for olive oil instead.

• Artichokes are the holy grail of Roman cuisine. Italian artichokes are small and violet, and have no discernible choke. Here is a stress-free way to clean them:

Cut a lemon in two and literally dip your fingertips in one half—this will prevent them from getting stained. Alternatively, wear disposable rubber gloves. Half-fill a medium bowl with water and squeeze in the juice of the other half of the lemon. Snap off the tough green outer leaves of the artichoke, until you reach the tender yellow and violet leaves. Using a small sharp knife, cut off all but 1 1/2 inches of the stem, then trim the bright green skin off of the base of the artichoke, using a spiral movement from the bottom to the top of the stem, until you get a rose shape. Cut off the top one-third of the artichoke (the pointy end). Brush the cut parts with lemon juice. If using large globe artichokes, you will need to remove the choke: grab the small, purple-tipped leaves at the center of the artichoke and pull them out, then scrape out the choke, making sure not to leave any of the hairy, fuzzy bits behind. Place the artichoke in the bowl of acidulated water to stop it from turning brown.

Chapter I
BREAKFAST RITUAL AL BAR

I've always been an early riser. Early mornings in Rome seem to contain a languorous secret: you have the city to yourself and you can hear the sound of your steps on the *sanpietrini* – the Roman cobblestones. Laid in order to lead pilgrims toward the Vatican, they have been polished to a shine by millions of pious feet. The downside is that they can become quite slippery, making them unsuitable for high speeds or high heels. The cobblestones are perfect, however, for those serendipitous meetings with a handsome stranger: you think you're gliding elegantly but stumble instead, ending up in a heap on the ground together with your shopping bags and your self-esteem.

At sunrise a peculiar crowd inhabits the city: garbage collectors, street artists, revelers making their way home, but not before indulging at a coffee bar. Most Italians rarely consider breakfast a meal; they simply make a quick stop at a café on their way to work, where they drink their coffee standing up, *al bar*. It'd be hard to imagine Italy without coffee. In fact, you could say *caffè* is the national breakfast. All Italians are coffee connoisseurs, even the ones who aren't. First they pay whichever member of the café-owner's family is behind the cash register that morning, then they take the receipt to the counter, and order their coffee. If the café has tables and chairs, the coffee you drink standing at the bar will cost much less than the one you drink sitting down.

But remember: when you order a *caffè* in Italy, it'll always means a *caffè espresso*. Do you fancy a change? Order a *caffè macchiato*, an espresso with a little bit of steamed milk in it, or a *caffè marocchino*, a macchiato with chocolate powder, or a *caffè Americano*, which is an espresso with a lot of hot water added to it. If you want more milk and more froth, order a *cappuccino*, but never, ever after breakfast time or you'll get some weird looks. If, however, you want to breakfast like a true Roman ask the barista for *"cappuccio e cornetto,"* a cappuccino and a croissant. Here the choices are endless: plain or with chocolate, filled with cream or jam. It could be a *bombolone* (the Italian version of a doughnut, *see* page 31), a cushiony *maritozzo* (*see* page 18), or a flaky *ventaglio* (*see* page 20) handed to you by the barista with a radiant smile. After that even the drabness of Monday morning won't look so bad.

Maritozzi

STICKY BUNS

The *maritozzo* is the centerpiece of my Roman breakfast. With its curious name—an affectionate derivative of *marito*, which means husband—it's a tease in the form of a sticky bun. It first became popular in the Middle Ages as a token of love, when the girl who made the most scrumptious *maritozzo* would gain the most delectable honor of all: the attention of the most beautiful young man in the neighborhood. Now, who wouldn't want to give that a try? Falling for such a deliciously tempting treat is as easy as falling in love for the first time.

Preparation time: 30 minutes plus rising

Cooking time: 20 minutes

Makes 8 *maritozzi*

1 teaspoon fast-acting dry yeast

1 cup lukewarm water, divided

1 teaspoon malt extract or superfine sugar

3 cups very strong white bread flour made from Canadian wheat, plus extra if necessary

1/3 cup superfine sugar

pinch of salt

1/4 cup corn oil

zest of 1 lemon

2 eggs, separated

2 tablespoons raisins, soaked in warm water for 10 minutes and drained

2 1/2 tablespoons pine nuts

zest of 1 orange

Sugar syrup:

2/3 cup white sugar

1/3 cup water

Filling:

1 1/2 cups heavy whipping cream

1/4 cup unsifted confectioners' sugar

1/2 cup pistachio nut kernels, crushed to a fine powder

Dissolve the yeast in 3 tablespoons of the measured water, add the malt extract, and mix well.

In a bowl, mix together the flour and sugar. Make a well in the center, add the yeast and malt mixture, and stir everything together.

In a separate bowl, add the salt, corn oil, and lemon zest to the remaining water and stir together, then pour the liquid over the flour mixture, add the egg yolks, and knead together to form a firm dough. Add the raisins, pine nuts, and orange zest to the dough and continue to knead until all the ingredients are well combined.

Dust the dough and bowl with a little flour, cover with plastic wrap, and let stand to rise in a warm place for at least 2 hours, or until it has risen by about one-third.

Transfer the risen dough onto a floured work surface and knead it for a couple of minutes, adding a little more flour if necessary, to obtain a firm and elastic dough. Divide the dough into eight pieces, then shape each piece into a round bun. Arrange the *maritozzi* on a cookie sheet lined with parchment paper, cover with plastic wrap, and let rest for another 30 minutes.

Once the buns have rested, shape them into ovals and brush them with the egg white. Cover them again with plastic wrap and let them to rise for 1 hour.

While the *maritozzi* are rising, preheat the oven to 350°F and prepare the sugar syrup. Heat the sugar and water in a saucepan over medium heat for 3 to 5 minutes without stirring until the liquid becomes transparent. Set aside to cool.

Bake the *maritozzi* for 20 minutes, or until golden brown, then remove them from the oven and brush with the sugar syrup. Let them cool on the cookie sheet for at least 20 minutes.

For the filling, beat the cream together with the confectioners' sugar until stiff peaks form. Make a cut lengthwise along each *maritozzo*, fill each with the whipped cream, and scatter with crushed pistachios. Heaven in a bun.

FLAKY PASTRY FANS

As soon as May arrives, Rome becomes ragingly hot. In the past, when gentlemen sought to escape the oppressive heat at festivities dedicated to Bacchus, the Roman god of wine and intoxication, they would find a quiet spot to be fanned by pretty girls with ostrich feather fans. In the Renaissance era, fans were a staple of the female costume—Lucrezia Borgia apparently had a collection of them—and feathers, ivory, and precious metals were the norm, tailor-made to satisfy any whim. Whatever the shape of the fan, it served as a tool of seduction during social events—when it was not being used as a fly swatter, of course.

Fragrant and sweet-scented, these lovely flaky fans are the epitome of Roman morning delights. Store them in an airtight container and they'll last for up to five days.

Preparation time: 10 minutes plus chilling

Cooking time: 20 minutes

Serves 6

1 x 11½-oz all-butter puff pastry sheet, thawed if frozen

½ cup light brown sugar, not packed

zest of 1 lemon

⅓ cup superfine sugar

Preheat the oven to 350°F. Line a cookie sheet with nonstick parchment paper.

Unroll the puff pastry sheet and sprinkle it with the brown sugar and lemon zest to coat the surface evenly.

Starting from one of the shorter sides, tightly roll the pastry into the middle, being careful not to tear it as you go. Repeat from the opposite side, leaving you with two adjoined tight pastry rolls. Loosely wrap the pastry in parchment paper and place it in the freezer for 15 minutes to firm up (this will make it easier to cut).

After 15 minutes, remove the pastry from the freezer and cut it widthwise into ½-inch slices. Tip the superfine sugar into a bowl and dip each slice into it to ensure they are completely coated on both sides.

Arrange the pastry fans on the prepared cookie sheet, being sure to leave at least 1 inch of space around each. Bake for 20 minutes, turning the cookie sheet around after 10 minutes, until golden brown and cooked through. Remove from the oven and transfer to a wire rack to cool before serving.

GRANOLA

In a city of excess, where showgirls can be elected to parliament but the average graduate is lucky to get an underpaid job, you might sometimes feel that the world is going crazy and that you are surrounded by nutjobs. Don't worry—at least this granola is full of the good kind of nuts. What I love about this recipe is that you can tailor it to your own taste, using whatever dried fruit, nuts, or tasty bits and pieces take your fancy. This breakfast will give you a soft yet energetic start to the day. Go nuts for the nuts.

Preparation time: 5 minutes plus soaking

Cooking time: 30 minutes

Makes about 1lb 14oz

2/3 cup raisins, not packed

1 cup whole almonds

3/4 cup pumpkin seeds

3/4 cup sunflower seeds

33/4 cups rolled oats

1 cup dried apricots, chopped

3 tablespoons maple syrup

3 tablespoons liquid wildflower honey

Preheat the oven to 300°F. Line a baking pan with nonstick parchment paper.

Place the raisins in a small bowl of water and let soak for 30 minutes, then drain and squeeze them dry with your hands.

Mix the rest of the dry ingredients together in a bowl. Add the maple syrup and honey and mix everything together well.

Spread the granola out in an even layer on the prepared baking pan and bake for 30 minutes, giving the pan a shake every so often and adding the raisins halfway through cooking, until crisp and evenly browned.

Remove the pan from the oven and use the end of a rolling pin to break the granola up into bite-sized pieces. Let cool before storing in an airtight container for up to 15 days.

Treccia di brioche con scaglie di cioccolato

BRIOCHE BRAID WITH CHOCOLATE FLAKES

Rome is the city with the most churches in the world—on a bright, pristine morning you can spy their cupolas from rooftop terraces with views as far as the eye can see. The history of the dome has accompanied the city for seventeen centuries, marking religious, social, and artistic evolutions. Today, the central dome of St. Peter's Basilica still dominates the Roman horizon. The domes rising from this fabulously soft bread look like little cupolas. This breakfast delight takes some time to prepare, but its beauty is hard to beat, like the view on the threshold of another dimension.

Preparation time: 20 minutes plus rising

Cooking time: 25 to 30 minutes

Makes 1 x 2lb loaf

4 cups bread flour

1 teaspoon fast-acting dry yeast

$1/4$ cup superfine sugar

4 eggs, beaten, plus 1 egg yolk

pinch of salt

6 cardamom pods, seeds extracted and ground

$13/4$ sticks unsalted butter, diced

$13/4$oz good-quality baker's chocolate (70% cocoa solids), broken into approximately $1/2$-inch squares

4 soft dried whole apricots, cut into quarters

2 tablespoons milk

3 teaspoons black poppy seeds

Line a 2-pound loaf pan (measuring $9^{1}/_{2}$ x $5^{1}/_{2}$ x $2^{1}/_{2}$ inches) with nonstick parchment paper.

Sift the flour, yeast, and sugar into a large mixing bowl or the bowl of an electric stand mixer fitted with the dough hook, tip in the beaten eggs, and knead together for 15 minutes, adding the salt, cardamom, and diced butter, a little at a time, to form a firm yet elastic dough. Transfer the dough to a bowl, cover with plastic wrap, and let rise in a warm place for 2 hours, or until doubled in size.

Knock the air out of the dough by lightly punching it back with your fists until it is smooth, then divide it in half. Divide each half into eight equal-sized pieces, shape into balls, and insert a square of chocolate and an apricot quarter into each, folding the dough around to make sure the filling is fully enclosed in the dough.

Arrange the dough balls in a tightly packed, even layer in the prepared loaf pan. Cover loosely with aluminum foil and let rise for another 2 hours.

Preheat the oven to 350°F.

Beat the egg yolk together with the milk and brush the mixture over the surface of the bread. Scatter with the poppy seeds and bake for 25 to 30 minutes, until the loaf is lightly golden and sounds hollow when removed from the pan and tapped on the bottom. Let the loaf rest for 5 minutes, then remove from the pan, transfer to a wire rack to cool, and serve.

UGLY BUT GOOD COOKIES

If not all that glitters is gold, the opposite is also true. It is maddening how some of Italy's greatest gastronomic delights look paradoxically unappealing. Take these cookies, for example, which resemble little mushy monsters. They are neither chromatically synchronized, nor are they balanced in terms of calorie versus fat intake. However, their color reminds me of the generously fertile soil of my beloved Italy, and beauty is in the eye of the beholder, after all.

Preparation time: 20 minutes

Cooking time: 15 minutes

Makes 40 cookies

$1/3$ cup water

1 teaspoon clear liquid honey

$2^{1}/2$ cups confectioners' sugar, divided

$1^{1}/4$ cups whole blanched hazelnuts, divided

1 cup almonds, divided

4 egg whites

pinch of salt

$1/4$ cup pomegranate seeds

Preheat the oven to 350°F. Line a cookie sheet with nonstick parchment paper.

Gently heat the measured water, honey, and $1/2$ cup of the sifted confectioners' sugar in a small saucepan until the sugar has dissolved. Remove from the heat and let cool.

Tip half the hazelnuts and almonds into a food processor and whiz together briefly until coarsely chopped.

Whisk the egg whites together with the salt in a bowl, until stiff peaks form. Continue to whisk, gradually adding the cooled sugar syrup and the remaining confectioners' sugar, little by little, for a further 10 minutes until glossy and firm.

Add the chopped nuts to the egg whites, folding them in gently with a metal spoon from bottom to top to prevent any air from escaping. Fold in the remaining whole nuts.

Use two teaspoons to shape $1/2$-inch balls of the mixture and arrange these on the lined cookie sheet in rows spaced $1/2$ inch apart. Scatter a few pomegranate seeds onto each cookie and bake for 15 minutes, until golden brown and crisp. Let cool. These can be stored in a sealed airtight container for up to 10 days.

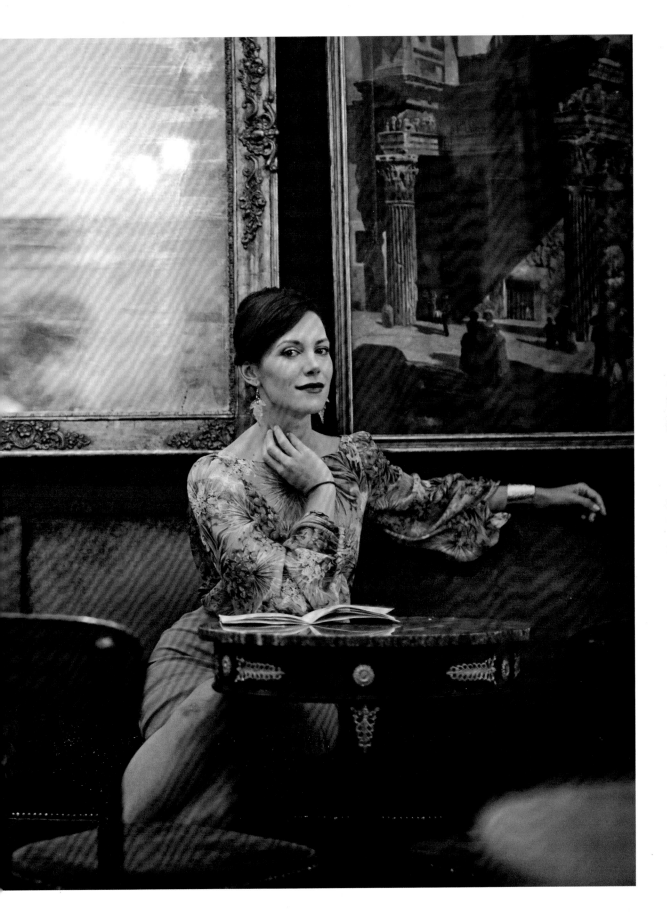

Bignè di San Giuseppe

ST. JOSEPH'S DAY CREAM PUFFS

Around mid-March and throughout the Carnival season, all the *pasticcerie* in town announce the impending arrival of *il bignè di San Giuseppe*. The color of the "Golden Tiber," this fried puff pastry is filled with a thrilling cream that tastes like ambrosia. A cream-smudged nose and a satisfied soul will be the result of tasting these captivating delights. They call my name from the shop window, and I always buy more than I should. You can adapt this recipe to make *pastarelle*, which are made all year round—simply halve the size of each *bignè*.

Preparation time: 30 minutes plus cooling

Cooking time: 20 to 30 minutes

Makes about 10 *bignè*

3/4 cup milk

3/4 cup water

1 stick unsalted butter, softened and diced

1 teaspoon superfine sugar

1 teaspoon salt

1 1/2 cups all-purpose flour

zest of 1 orange

2 eggs

vegetable oil, for frying (optional)

1 cup sifted confectioners' sugar

Custard:

1/3 cup superfine sugar

6 egg yolks

3 cups milk

1/3 cup all-purpose flour

zest of 1 lemon

Icing:

3 tablespoons water

2/3 cup confectioners' sugar

dash of pink, yellow, or blue food coloring (optional)

For the custard, mix together the sugar and egg yolks in a saucepan, then add the milk, flour, and lemon zest. Heat gently, stirring continuously, until the mixture starts to bubble. Let simmer for 2 to 3 minutes then transfer to a bowl and let cool. Cover with plastic wrap and set aside.

In a heavy saucepan, stir together the milk, measured water, butter, sugar, and salt over medium-low heat. Cook, stirring, for 1 to 2 minutes until the mixture is thick and creamy. Sift in the flour, add the orange zest, and stir quickly and continuously to form a smooth ball of dough that comes away from the inside of the pan. Tip the dough into a bowl and let cool for 10 minutes before beating in the eggs.

Cut out a rectangle of nonstick parchment paper measuring 9 1/2 x 7 inches, then cut this into about 10 squares. Using two tablespoons or a pastry bag, form round fig-sized mounds of the pastry on top of each square.

To fry the *bignè*, half-fill a large pot or deep-fryer with vegetable oil and heat to 350°F, or until a cube of bread dropped in the oil browns in 30 seconds. Carefully lower the *bignè*, each still attached to its paper square (these will come off after a few seconds and can be removed with tongs) into the hot oil and fry for 1 to 2 minutes until golden on all sides. Remove the pastries with a slotted spoon and drain them on a plate lined with paper towels. Dust them generously with the confectioners' sugar.

Alternatively, for a healthier version, preheat the oven to 350°F. Arrange the *bignè* on their paper squares on a cookie sheet, dust them generously with confectioners' sugar, and bake for about 25 minutes, until golden.

Once the pastries have cooked and cooled, carefully make a hole at the bottom of each. Use a pastry bag to fill the *bignè* with the custard.

For the icing, bring the measured water to a boil in a small saucepan and add the confectioners' sugar a tablespoon at a time, stirring constantly to dissolve, until the mixture is smooth and all the sugar has been incorporated. For a colored glaze, add a few drops of food coloring.

Smear the top of each *bignè* with a teaspoon or so of the icing and refrigerate until ready to serve.

Bomboloni
BAKED DOUGHNUTS

As a child, I used to be a doughnut queen, slipping them on my fingers as symbols of my power (the power of being a pest!). Now that I'm a grown-up, well most of the time, I like to let the aroma of freshly baked doughnuts float me into consciousness, reassuring me that all is well with the world as I wake up. A little voluptuous recklessness, and I'm ready for the day ahead. In this recipe I use instant mashed potato flakes in order to create an extra-moist doughnut. If you don't have mashed potato flakes in your cupboard, you can substitute the real thing instead.

Preparation time: 20 minutes plus rising

Cooking time: 15 minutes

Makes 20 *bomboloni*

1 cup milk, divided

1¼ cups instant mashed potato flakes

1 teaspoon fast-acting dry yeast

2 cups all-purpose flour, plus extra for dusting

2 cups very strong white bread flour, made from Canadian wheat

3 eggs, plus 1 beaten egg yolk for brushing

½ cup superfine sugar, plus extra for dusting

¾ stick softened unsalted butter, plus extra, melted, for brushing

zest of 1 orange

zest of 1 lemon

Line a baking pan with nonstick parchment paper.

In a small bowl, mix together ⅔ cup of the milk with the potato flakes until thick and creamy.

In a separate bowl, dissolve the yeast in the remaining milk.

Sift the flours into a large mixing bowl or the bowl of an electric stand mixer fitted with the dough hook and add the potato mixture, yeast mixture, and all the remaining ingredients. Knead for 15 minutes to form a soft dough that comes away from the inside of the bowl.

Place the dough in a large bowl, cover with a clean dish cloth, and set aside in a warm place to prove for 2 to 3 hours, or until the dough has tripled in size.

Roll the dough out on a lightly floured work surface to a ½-inch thickness. Using a 3½-inch floured doughnut cutter, cut out 20 doughnuts. Alternatively, if you don't have a doughnut cutter, try using the rim of an old-fashioned glass, flouring it as you go, to cut out 20 circles, then use the rim of a regular shot glass to remove the dough from the center of each circle to form the holes.

Carefully place the doughnuts on the prepared baking pan, making sure to leave at least 1 inch between them. Cover the doughnuts with a dish cloth and let stand to prove for a further 30 minutes.

Preheat the oven to 350°F.

Brush the proved doughnuts with egg wash and bake for 10 to 15 minutes until golden. Remove from the oven and brush with a little melted butter, then dust generously with sugar. Serve warm or cold.

Biscottoni da inzuppo

DUNKING BISCOTTI

Although I didn't know it at the time, it was in my grandmother's pantry, that exuberant temple of gluttony, that a sort of initiation to what would become an existence of utter gratification through the joys of food first occurred. Moist, nutty, and simple, these exquisite biscotti hold all the nostalgic splendor that I associate with childhood. I love to dip them in my cappuccino or crumble them over plain yogurt in the morning. And wherever I am in the world, whenever I taste a biscotti echoing with this aroma, I know I'm home.

Preparation time: 15 minutes plus cooling

Cooking time: 20 to 25 minutes

Makes 30 biscotti

butter, for greasing

4 cups super-fine grade 00 pasta flour, plus extra for dusting

1 teaspoon baking soda

1 teaspoon cream of tartar

1¼ cups superfine sugar, plus 2½ tablespoons extra for dusting

3 large eggs, plus 1 beaten egg for brushing

½ cup milk

½ teaspoon baking powder

½ cup extra virgin olive oil

Preheat the oven to 350°F. Grease a large ladyfinger mold (or an eclair pan) or a cookie sheet with butter and dust it with flour.

Put the flour in a bowl with the baking soda, cream of tartar, and sugar. Crack in the eggs and beat together until pale and fluffy.

Gently warm the milk in a saucepan, then remove from the heat, add the baking powder, and stir to dissolve. Tip the warm milk into the egg mixture and stir to combine before adding the oil and working everything together to form a wet, spongy dough.

Fill the prepared ladyfinger mold with the dough, gently pressing and patting the dough into each mold to ensure a neat shape. Alternatively, use a pastry bag to pipe the dough onto the cookie sheet into rectangles measuring 4 x ¾-inches, leaving at least ½ inch between each piece. Brush with the beaten egg and bake for 10 to 15 minutes. Remove from the oven and dust with superfine sugar, then bake for a further 5 to 10 minutes until the biscotti are golden on top and firm to the touch. Let cool on a wire rack for at least 30 minutes, preferably overnight, before storing in an airtight container for up to 2 months. Serve with coffee or cold milk for dunking.

Fette biscottate

SWEET MELBA TOAST

There are times—especially when I'm trying to stick to my New Year's resolutions—when I allow myself fewer treats, but these crackling melba toasts are always among them. Irresistibly golden and crisp, they find their perfect match in homemade seasonal jam, but I also enjoy them more ascetically, just on their own, without all the colorful clamor that I usually associate with Rome.

Preparation time: 15 minutes plus rising

Cooking time: 1¾ hours

Makes 15 to 20 pieces

1½ sticks softened unsalted butter, plus extra for greasing

½ cup milk

1 x ¼-oz package of fast-acting dry yeast

2 tablespoons brown sugar, divided

½ cup lukewarm water

4 cups bread flour, made from Canadian wheat

3 large eggs, plus 1 beaten egg for brushing

1 teaspoon salt

⅓ cup flaxseeds

Butter and line a 9-inch loaf pan with nonstick parchment paper. In a small pan, heat the milk gently until lukewarm.

Add the yeast and half the sugar to the measured water in a bowl and stir together to dissolve.

Sift the flour into a separate bowl or the bowl of an electric stand mixer fitted with the dough hook. Making a well in the center, add the dissolved yeast mixture, eggs, remaining sugar, and warm milk. Knead well for about 10 minutes to form a smooth, elastic dough, then add the salt, flaxseeds, and softened butter, little by little, until it is fully incorporated. Knead for a further 5 minutes. Roll the dough into a ball, cover the bowl with a clean dish cloth, and let rise in a warm place for 45 minutes, or until doubled in size.

Taking the dough in your hands, shape it to approximately the size of the prepared loaf pan. Gently lower the dough into the pan and let it rise for a further hour. Don't worry about the dough overhanging the pan; it will make for beautifully shaped toasts.

Preheat the oven to 350°F.

Brush the dough with the beaten egg and bake for 45 minutes, or until the loaf is lightly golden and sounds hollow when removed from the pan and tapped on the bottom. Remove the loaf from the pan and let cool on a wire rack for 1 hour.

Once cool, slice the loaf into approximately ½-inch pieces—you can slice them thicker or thinner depending on personal taste. Arrange the slices on a cookie sheet lined with parchment paper and bake at 300°F for a further hour, at the end of which they'll be dry and golden. Transfer the toast to a wire rack and let cool before sealing them in an airtight container, where they will last for up to 1 week.

Budini di riso

RICE PUDDING TARTLETS

Trastevere, where I got this recipe, is the undisputed street-food center of Rome. It is also home to the most outspoken Roman *matrone*, who treat each meal with a solemn sense of ceremony. The true food connoisseur knows that these formidable Roman women were dictating food trends when celebrity chefs were still in diapers. They would never go to a supermarket filled with convenience foods—you'll only find them shopping at the local market, spreading their unshakable opinions on today's customs. "EAT!" they command if you sit at their table. That's how I grew up, and why I made it a rule to go jogging twice a week. These tartlets are full of Italian *mamma* warmth and spiky charm. Wait until the rice turns translucent and creamy, then pour it into the pastry crusts. This dish is like the Romans: a bit hard on the outside, but with a tremendous amount of heart.

Preparation time: 15 minutes plus chilling

Cooking time: 60 minutes

Makes 12 tartlets

$4\frac{1}{3}$ cups milk

zest of 1 lemon

1 tablespoon vanilla extract or 1 vanilla bean, split lengthwise and seeds scraped

$1\frac{1}{2}$ cups carnaroli or arborio risotto rice

$\frac{1}{3}$ cup light brown sugar, divided

2 teaspoons baking powder

2 large eggs, separated

pinch of salt

Pastry:

$\frac{3}{4}$ cup all-purpose flour

1 cup wholemeal spelt flour

$\frac{2}{3}$ cup rice flour

$\frac{1}{3}$ cup turbinado sugar

pinch of salt

2 teaspoons baking powder

$1\frac{1}{2}$ sticks cold unsalted butter, diced

1 large egg

Line 12 holes of a muffin pan with nonstick paper baking cups.

For the pastry, sift the three flours into a large bowl and mix together with the sugar, salt, and baking powder. Add the butter and stir together with a wooden spoon to form a crumbly dough. (Try not to touch the butter with your hands or it will melt, making for a soggy pastry.)

Beat the egg in a bowl, add it to the dough, and mix everything together until smooth. Roll the dough into a ball, seal it in plastic wrap, and let it rest in the refrigerator for 1 hour.

Pour the milk into a large heavy saucepan, add the lemon zest and vanilla extract or seeds, and bring to a simmer. When it starts bubbling, add the rice and cook for 20 to 30 minutes, or following the package directions, until the rice is soft and creamy. Remove from the heat, add half the brown sugar, and let cool.

Preheat the oven to 340°F.

When the rice has cooled completely, stir in the baking powder, egg yolks, and remaining sugar.

In a separate bowl, whip the egg whites with a pinch of salt until firm, then fold them delicately into the rice pudding.

Divide the dough into 12 equal-sized pieces. Taking one piece, gently press the pastry with your fingers into one of the paper baking cups in the muffin pan to make a crust. Repeat with the remaining pastry pieces.

Spoon the rice pudding into the pastry crusts and bake about 40 minutes, or until the rice tartlets are golden brown around the edges. Remove from the oven and serve warm or cold, with a dusting of confectioners' sugar or some fresh fruit and yogurt.

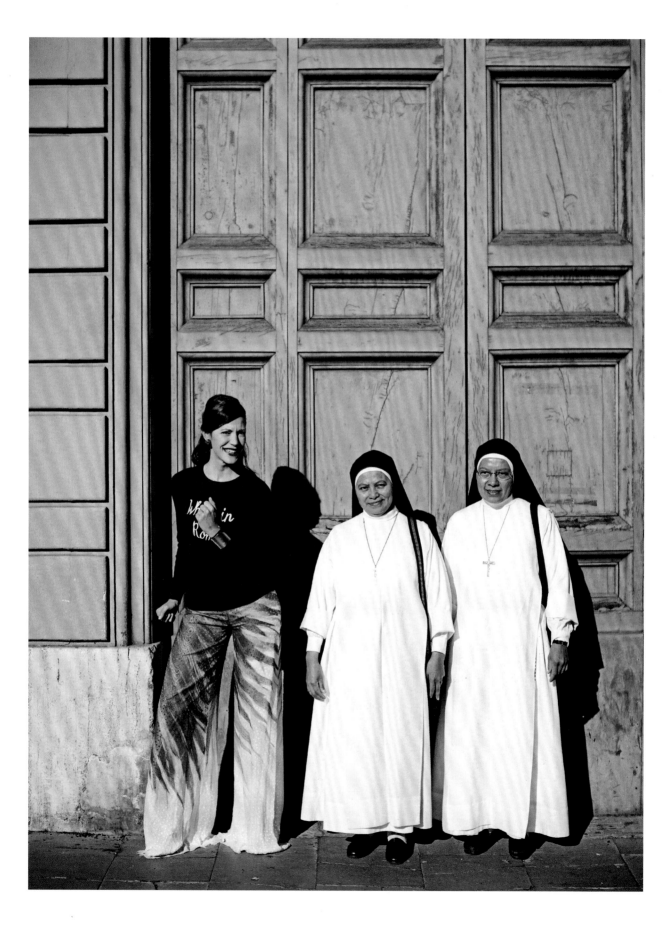

Chapter 2 MERENDE

"Che ne voi artri du' chicchetti?" — "Why don't you have a couple more mouthfuls?" was the question those tall women piously dressed in black would always ask in the canteen of my Roman Catholic elementary school. The nun who introduced me to a love for everything that smells good and tastes comforting was called Suor Fortunata. An abundance of flesh, eau de Cologne, and sweets were her particular traits, along with a liberal use of guilt as an educational tool. When school was out for the summer, I would hop on a bus filled with screaming children. Destination: summer camp. This would usually be held in one of the many medieval monasteries dotted around the Roman countryside, and yet it would always take no less than four hours to get there. Was it the magic of the packed school bus or the voice of Suor Beata (Blessed Sister—could you ever compete with that ethereal grace?) reverberating with flinty humor that slowed time down to a crawl? I couldn't tell.

In the afternoons, we would furtively run to the pantry to indulge in some crunchy *ovis molis* (*see* page 57) or *pizzette rosse* (*see* page 55). As soon as a nun arrived, however, we would hide behind the extra-large jar filled with *tarallucci* (*see* page 43), since we knew that anyone caught helping themselves to a *merenda* or snack before dinner time, thereby violating the sanctity of the meal, would be in big trouble.

Everyone had to help prepare the evening meal: one of us would peel the potatoes, another would crack eggs into a dish to prepare the *costolette* (breaded veal chops). This ritual, which I now habitually recreate in my own life by enlisting the help of friends and family in the kitchen, was a sort of sumptuous confessional. The handling of all this food punctuated our personalities, which emerged through telling stories and cracking jokes. It created intimacy.

Those sweet-tempered, indefatigable, often mustachioed women taught me how to recognize the best produce and to respect every season. Many churches in Rome and beyond still boast a *hortum botanicum*, a lovingly tended vegetable garden, the congregation's pride and joy, which according to the season provides a bountiful supply of cabbages, tomatoes, endives, radishes, eggplant, potatoes, bell peppers, and more.

Tarallucci al vino

BAKED SWEET WINE PRETZELS

The walls of Fiaschetteria Beltramme, a restaurant on Via della Croce, are lined with rows of 19th-century *fiaschi*—traditional straw-wrapped wine bottles. The villages of the Castelli Romani area, from Ariccia, where *porchetta* (*see* page 188) comes from, to Tivoli, home to the splendid Villa Adriana, all have one thing in common: their soft, unfussy wine. What bliss to have your drink served with these crisp, wine-flavored little snacks!

Tarallucci are also a perfect mood raiser for your mid-morning coffee break. They are traditionally made with sambuca (*see* page 271) and the kind of wine everyone despises because "you can taste the cork." This recipe is a perfect way to put it to good use, since throwing it away would be a sin in Italian *cucina povera* culture, where nothing is wasted.

Preparation time: 20 minutes

Cooking time: 20 minutes

Makes 40 *tarallucci*

3 cups all-purpose flour, plus extra for dusting

pinch of salt

2 tablespoons anise seeds

1/2 cup extra virgin olive oil

1 1/3 cups light brown sugar, not packed, divided, plus extra for glazing

1/2 cup red wine

1 tablespoon Roman-style Sambuca (*see* page 271), Grand Marnier, or other herb-based liqueur

Preheat the oven to 350°F. Line a large baking pan with parchment paper.

Put the flour, salt, anise seeds, oil, and half the sugar into a bowl and mix together well. Gradually add the wine and sambuca and keep mixing to form a firm dough.

Divide the dough into 40 equal-sized pieces. Take a piece and shape it into a ball, then, using the palms of your hands, roll it out on a floured surface into a thin rope about 4 inches long. Bring the ends together to form a ring (don't worry if it isn't quite a perfect circle—it's fine if it looks more like a teardrop). Repeat with the rest of the dough pieces.

Put the remaining brown sugar into a bowl and dip the dough rings into the sugar to coat them completely. Arrange the *tarallucci* on the prepared baking pan, leaving 1/2 inch between them, and bake for 20 minutes or until golden brown.

Let the *tarallucci* cool on a wire rack for 2 hours before serving.

Insalata di farro con pollo, zucchine e formaggio di capra

SPELT SALAD WITH CHICKEN, ZUCCHINI & GOAT CHEESE

When I put my New Year's resolutions into practice, I start the day with a cup of hot water and lemon juice. Later on I make this wonderfully light, tasty recipe that catches the flavors of my Rome. Not that I should be feeling smug, because this is incredibly quick and easy. With a delicious nutty taste, spelt is easier to digest than more common types of wheat. This dish is therefore also perfect for a date, since no one wants to be romantic on a heavy stomach. This recipe is just a starting point: feel free to use any ingredients that take your fancy.

Preparation time: 10 minutes plus soaking

Cooking time: 25 minutes

Serves 2

3 tablespoons raisins

3/4 cup pearled spelt or pearl barley

small handful of sea salt flakes

1/4 cup extra virgin olive oil, divided

3 1/2oz chicken breast, cut into 1/2-inch strips

1 zucchini, halved lengthwise and very finely sliced

8 cherry tomatoes, cut into 1/4-inch cubes

3 1/2oz semisoft goat cheese, cut into 1/4-inch cubes

3 1/2oz arugula, coarsely chopped

zest and juice of 1 lemon

small handful of chopped mint leaves

Place the raisins in a small bowl of water and let soak for 30 minutes, then drain and squeeze them dry with your hands.

Place the spelt in a large saucepan, cover with water, and bring to a boil. Add the sea salt flakes and cook following the package directions until the spelt is fluffy but still retains a bit of crunch (this usually takes about 15 to 18 minutes). Once cooked, drain the spelt and pass it under cold running water to cool it and stop it from cooking further. Transfer to a large bowl and set aside.

Heat 1 tablespoon of olive oil in a ridged grill pan or nonstick skillet until smoking hot, then add the chicken and zucchini strips and cook for 3 minutes on each side, brushing with the oil as you go, until the chicken is cooked through. Remove from the heat and set aside.

Add the tomatoes, goat cheese, raisins, and arugula to the spelt. Drizzle with the remaining olive oil and season with salt, then scatter with the lemon zest and sprinkle with the lemon juice. Add the mint leaves and mix together well so that everything is evenly coated in the dressing. Pile the chicken and zucchini strips on top of the salad to serve.

Trio di bruschette

THREE BRUSCHETTE OF A KIND

Literally meaning "roasted," *bruschetta* is how farmers traditionally savored bread—rubbed with garlic and seasoned with olive oil and salt. I love this dish: it puts me back in touch with the most authentic part of me. Each season has its own favorite topping combination, so get ready to free your imagination and enjoy the intensity of these mouthwatering morsels!

Preparation time: 10 minutes

Cooking time: 25 minutes

Makes 15 *bruschette*

1 rustic bread loaf, cut into slices ½ inch thick

20 Marinated Anchovies or Sardines (*see* page 147)

Tomato and eggplant topping:

2 tablespoons extra virgin olive oil

1 garlic clove, peeled and left whole

1 small eggplant, cut into ¼-inch chunks

2 cherry tomatoes, cut into ¼-inch chunks

3 tablespoons white wine

5 sage leaves, chopped

salt

Sausage and broccolini topping:

1 pork sausage

1 cup broccolini florets

2 tablespoons extra virgin olive oil

1 teaspoon fennel seeds

For the tomato and eggplant topping, heat the oil in a nonstick skillet. Lightly crush the garlic clove with the flat side of a heavy knife blade, add to the skillet, and fry it gently until golden. Remove the garlic clove from the pan, add the eggplant and tomato pieces, and season with salt. Increase the heat to medium-high, add the wine, and cook, stirring, for about 10 minutes, or until the wine has evaporated and the eggplant is tender. Scatter with the sage leaves and set aside.

For the sausage and broccolini topping, squeeze the sausage out of its casing and cook in a small nonstick skillet, breaking the meat up with a wooden spoon and stirring occasionally to prevent it from sticking to the dry pan, until cooked through. Bring a small pan of salted water to a boil, add the broccolini, and cook for 5 minutes, then drain and transfer to the pan with the sausage. Add the oil and fennel seeds and continue to cook, stirring, for 5 minutes, to allow the flavors to mingle. Set aside.

Preheat the broiler to medium–high.

Arrange the bread slices on an cookie sheet and place under the broiler for 5 minutes until lightly golden. Transfer to a serving plate and divide the tomato and eggplant, the sausage and broccolini, and the marinated anchovy or sardine toppings evenly between the slices and serve.

Torta rustica carciofi, piselli e prosciutto

SAVORY PIE WITH ARTICHOKES, PEAS & HAM

White bread has always been associated with wealth, whereas dark bread was typical of simple country living. In 1870, a wave of country dwellers moved to Rome, Italy's newly elected capital. Wholewheat bread went out of fashion as people tried to emulate the lifestyle of the upper classes. But food trends are cyclical, so this humble dish is back in the spotlight. This fabulously healthy pie is what I turn to when an unexpected craving hits me in the middle of the day. And no, you can't have too much of this good thing.

Preparation time: 15 minutes plus chilling

Cooking time: $1\frac{1}{4}$ hours

Serves 8

3 tablespoons extra virgin olive oil, plus extra for brushing

1 garlic clove, peeled and left whole

3 artichokes, cleaned (*see* page 13), quartered lengthwise, and placed in acidulated water

1 cup garden peas, defrosted if frozen

small handful of mint leaves, finely sliced

2 tablespoons water

14oz *mozzarella da cucina* (cooking mozzarella)

$\frac{1}{4}$ cup bread crumbs (*see* page 262)

7oz roast ham, cut into $\frac{1}{8}$-inch strips

salt

Pastry:

$1\frac{2}{3}$ cups bread flour

2 cups rye flour

$\frac{1}{4}$ cup white wine

pinch of salt

approximately $\frac{1}{4}$ cup water

small handful of basil leaves

For the pastry, stir together the flours, wine, and salt in a large bowl together with enough water (about $\frac{1}{4}$ cup) to form a sticky dough. Add the basil and continue to mix together until smooth. Place the dough in a bowl, cover with a dish cloth, and let rest in the refrigerator for 30 minutes.

Preheat the oven to 350°F.

Heat the oil in a large nonstick skillet, add the garlic clove, and fry it over low heat. When it starts to brown remove it from the pan. Add the artichokes and peas and cook over medium heat for 15 minutes until the vegetables have softened, adding the mint and water halfway through cooking. Season to taste and set aside.

Cut the mozzarella into approximately $\frac{1}{2}$-inch cubes and pat them dry with paper towels to remove any excess water. Mix the mozzarella pieces together with the bread crumbs to coat evenly.

Once chilled, roll three-quarters of the dough out with a rolling pin to a $\frac{1}{4}$-inch thickness. Cut out an 11-inch pastry circle and place it in the bottom of a 10-inch pie plate, leaving the excess overhanging. Cut the remaining dough into seven strips, each $1\frac{1}{2}$-inches wide.

Prick the pastry in the pie plate with a fork, then cover it with the ham, artichokes, peas, and crumbed mozzarella pieces. Arrange the pastry strips across the surface in a criss-cross lattice pattern, fold in the overhanging dough, and seal the edges well. Brush with a little oil, cover with a sheet of parchment paper, and bake for 30 minutes. Remove the parchment paper and bake for a further 30 minutes until the pastry is nicely golden. Enjoy hot or cold with a green salad or alongside a bowl of soup.

Tortino di verdure incartato

WRAPPED VEGETABLE PIE

With its exhilarating aroma and vivid flavor this is not your usual lasagne—instead of layers of egg pasta, here we use crunchy leaves of chard, giving this dish the appearance of a beautifully wrapped present. To me, herbs make up the personality traits of a dish. I like to use sage and basil here, but you can personalize this bewitching pie with any herb you fancy. Go on, make it yours.

Preparation time: 40 minutes

Cooking time: 1 hour 40 minutes

Serves 6

½ stick salted butter

1lb 2oz leeks, trimmed, cleaned, and finely sliced

handful of basil leaves, coarsely chopped

handful of sage leaves, coarsely chopped

1lb 2oz chard, trimmed and stalks separated

3 eggs

1 cup heavy whipping cream

1 carrot, cut into ¼-inch cubes

1 celery stalk, cut into ¼-inch cubes

7oz radishes

salt and pepper

Melt the butter in a large saucepan over very low heat, add the leeks, and cook gently, stirring occasionally, for 1 hour, until the leeks are soft, translucent, and falling apart. Stir in the basil and sage, season with salt and pepper, and remove from the heat. Set aside.

Meanwhile, put the chard pieces into a large pan of salted boiling water and blanch for 2 to 3 minutes. Drain and let dry between two clean dish cloths.

Preheat the oven to 350°F. Dampen a sheet of parchment paper with a little water and use it to line a 7-inch springform cake pan.

In a bowl, beat the eggs together until light and fluffy. Add the whipping cream and beat together until the mixture is slightly firm, then season with salt and pepper and stir in the sautéed leeks along with the carrot and celery cubes.

Arrange the dried chard pieces, reserving a handful, in an overlapping pattern to cover the bottom and sides of the prepared cake pan. Fill the pan with the cream and vegetable mixture, then cover with the remaining leaves, folding the overhanging leaves toward the middle like a parcel to enclose the filling. Loosely cover the *tortino* with parchment paper, and cook in the oven for 40 minutes until the filling has set firm.

Remove the *tortino* from the oven and gently flip it over, removing the parchment paper. Using a mandoline or sharp knife, cut the radishes into thin slices and use to decorate the top of the *tortino*. Serve hot or cold.

Pizzette rosse

MINI PIZZAS WITH TOMATO SAUCE

When it comes to the constant movie that is Rome, I like to take it in with all my senses alert.
I'll take some *pizzette rosse* with me for my mid-morning stroll around the market while
secretly people-watching. Eating while shopping for food: how very Roman!
These fragrant beauties are even more delicious eaten the next day. Just warm them up in the
oven at 225°F for five minutes for some comfort food at its tastiest.
I like to use a tiny espresso cup as a template for my mini pizzas, but you can also use
a cappuccino cup or a cereal bowl for a larger pizza thrill.

Preparation time: 10 minutes plus rising

Cooking time: 15 to 20 minutes

Makes about 40 *pizzette*

1 cup passata (sieved tomatoes)

small handful of basil leaves, chopped

2 tablespoons extra virgin olive oil

1 teaspoon salt

3¹/₂oz *mozzarella da cucina* (cooking mozzarella), cut into ¹/₄-inch cubes

Dough:

4 cups bread flour, plus extra for dusting

1 teaspoon superfine sugar

2 tablespoons fast-acting dry yeast

1 cup lukewarm water plus 3 tablespoons

2 tablespoons unsalted butter, softened

1 teaspoon extra virgin olive oil

1 teaspoon salt

To prepare the dough, sift the flour into a large mixing bowl with the sugar. Dissolve the yeast in 1 cup of lukewarm water, add it to the flour and sugar, and mix together for 5 minutes. Add the butter, oil, and salt and mix for a further 2 to 3 minutes to form a soft, sticky dough. Add up to 3 tablespoons more water as needed—the dough should feel neither sticky nor dry. Cover the bowl with a clean dish cloth and let rise in a warm place for 1 hour, or until almost doubled in size.

Preheat the oven to 400°F. Mix the passata, basil, oil, and salt together in a bowl and set aside.

To make the *pizzette*, roll out the risen dough on a clean, floured work surface to a thickness of ¹/₂ inch. Press down onto the surface of the dough with a small cup, glass, or bowl of your choice to form your pizzette disks. Spoon a little of the passata over the center of each *pizzetta*, being sure to leave the edges empty so that you have that typical white/red contrast of a good margherita pizza.

Cook in the oven for 15 to 20 minutes, adding a few mozzarella cubes to the top of each *pizzetta* halfway through cooking, until the cheese is bubbling and the *pizzetta* bases are crisp.

Girelle di pan carrè con mousse di prosciutto cotto agrumata

SANDWICH WHEELS WITH PROSCIUTTO MOUSSE

At art gallery openings in Rome, you can see people's eyes flicking toward the buffet during the speeches. Don't be fooled by their perfectly pressed suits and glamorous hairdos; their only real interest lies in eating as much free food as possible.

To enjoy this prosciutto mousse at its best, be sure to prepare it at least 12 hours before serving. As with everything in life, organization is key. That's why cooking, to me, is like therapy: when life gets tough, I can start with the tiny details in the kitchen. If I can be organized there, then there's hope for everything else.

Preparation time: 30 minutes plus chilling

Serves 20 as part of a canapé selection

2 fine gelatin leaves

½ cup heavy whipping cream

1lb 5oz smoked or roast ham, cut into ¼-inch cubes, divided

2 tablespoons French mustard

2 tablespoons tomato ketchup

15 black peppercorns

¼ cup lemon juice

4 lemons

1 sliced white bread loaf

1 sliced wholewheat bread loaf

Soak the gelatin leaves in a small bowl of lukewarm water for 5 minutes, then remove and squeeze out the excess water.

Bring a medium-sized saucepan half filled with water to a simmer. Whisk together the whipping cream and gelatin leaves in an ovenproof bowl that fits snugly over the pan until the gelatin has dissolved. Set aside over very low heat.

Reserve 3 ounces of the ham cubes and place the rest into a food processor together with the mustard, ketchup, peppercorns, and lemon juice. Blend together for 30 seconds to form a light, creamy paste. Add the warm cream and gelatin mixture and blend together for a further 30 seconds, then spoon the mousse into a large bowl and fold in the reserved ham cubes.

Wet a 6¼-inch square terrine mold under running water, then line it with a sheet of parchment paper. Fill the mold with the mousse, cover it with plastic wrap, and let chill in the refrigerator for at least 12 hours (preferably overnight) to set.

When you're ready to serve, halve the lemons and slice the halves as thinly as possible. Remove the crust from the bread slices and cut each slice into four pieces.

Spread a generous amount of the mousse on a bread slice quarter and roll it up into a coil. Place a slice of lemon on top of the rolled slice and skewer it with a toothpick to hold it in place. Repeat with the remaining ingredients, and arrange the sandwich wheels on a large serving platter to finish. Serve alongside a range of other nibbles (*see* pages 126–49).

Trio di ovis molis alle marmellate

SHORTBREAD COOKIE TRIO WITH JAM

The nuns at my school evangelized about a simpler way of life, where the only appropriate activities were prayer and tending the vegetable garden. *Ora et labora*. They would regularly pick the ingredients they needed in their kitchen garden—a cook's idea of heaven.

The best flavor combinations come from ingredients that grow together, so during jam-making season, peaches, apricots, and strawberries would make for a happy bunch. This trio of cookies makes my soul sparkle—the colors of the different types of jam, the confectioners' sugar dusted on top, and the soothing taste all combine to ensure great satisfaction.

Preparation time: 5 minutes plus cooling

Cooking time: 15 minutes

Makes about 20 cookies

⅓ cup sunflower seeds

¾ cup bread flour

½ cup confectioners' sugar, plus extra for dusting

¾ stick cold unsalted butter, diced

zest of 1 lemon

1 egg yolk

½ teaspoon baking powder

1 tablespoon each of your 3 favorite jams (I like apricot, peach, and strawberry)

20 raspberries (optional)

Preheat the oven to 350°F. Line a cookie sheet with nonstick parchment paper.

Tip the sunflower seeds into a clean coffee or spice grinder and grind to a fine powder.

Sift the flour into a bowl, add the confectioners' sugar, ground sunflower seeds, butter, lemon zest, egg yolk, and baking powder and mix everything together well to form a firm dough.

Divide the dough into 20 equal-sized balls. Using your thumb, press down on the center of each ball to create a dimple.

Arrange the cookies on the prepared cookie sheet and bake for 12 minutes until the cookies are slightly golden. Remove from the oven and let cool on a wire rack.

Meanwhile, gently heat your chosen jams in 3 separate small pans until liquid in consistency.

Once the cookies have cooled, spoon a little of your first hot jam into the dimples of one-third of the cookies. Repeat with the remaining jams and cookies. Top each cookie with a raspberry, if you like, and dust with confectioners' sugar to finish.

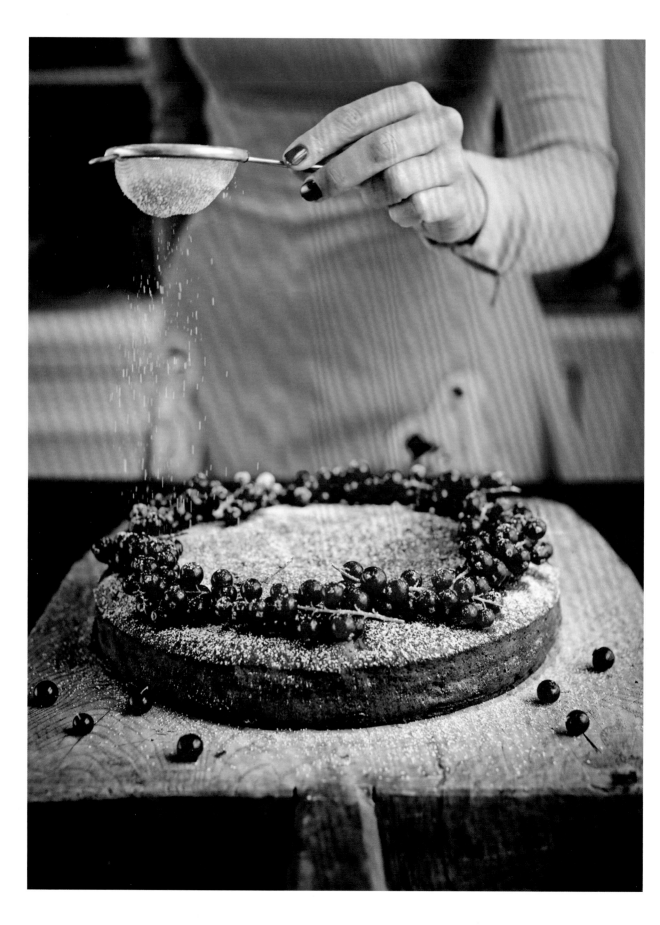

Ciambellone di polenta alla zucca e mele

POLENTA CAKE WITH PUMPKIN & APPLE

Rome is built on seven hills: Campidoglio, Celio, Esquilino, Palatino, Viminale, Quirinale, and Aventino. This last hill is the quieter one, with a solemn air. It also has an ace in the hole that I like to keep as a surprise when strolling through the city with non-Roman friends—the keyhole of the gate to the Priory of the Knights of Malta. Peep through it and you will enjoy a spellbinding view of the dome of St. Peter's, framed by the orange trees in the priory garden. This cake bursts with so much flavor that I can't help but be taken back to that magnificent garden in the summer, when the air is pervaded by the heady scent of ripe oranges. In this recipe, the polenta mixed together with earthy orange pumpkin purée and apples makes for a vibrant combination. Dizzyingly delicious.

Preparation time: 10 minutes plus soaking and cooling

Cooking time: 1 hour 50 minutes

Serves 10

unsalted butter, for greasing

4 cups all-purpose flour, plus extra for dusting

1 cup raisins, not packed

3 1/2 cups peeled pumpkin, cut into 2-inch cubes

2 Bramley or other cooking apples, peeled, cored, and diced

4 large eggs

2 cups superfine sugar

1/4 cup extra virgin olive oil

1 1/4 cups polenta (cornmeal) flour

2 teaspoons baking powder

1 tablespoon rum

zest of 1 orange

2 1/4 cups red currants

confectioner's sugar, to decorate

Preheat the oven to 400°F. Line a baking pan with nonstick parchment paper and grease a 13-inch springform cake pan (or ring cake pan) and dust it with flour.

Place the raisins in a small bowl of water and let soak for 30 minutes, then drain and squeeze them dry with your hands.

Meanwhile, arrange the pumpkin pieces on the prepared baking pan and bake for 40 minutes, or until soft. Remove from the oven and let cool for 10 minutes, then crush the pumpkin pieces with a fork to a rough purée-like consistency.

Tip the apple pieces into a saucepan, cover with water, and bring to a simmer. Cook over medium heat for about 10 minutes, until the apple pieces are soft and just starting to break down. Drain and set aside.

Beat the eggs together with the sugar in a large bowl until pale and fluffy. Beating continuously, gradually add the oil, then sift in the flours and baking powder, and mix together to form a batter. Add the rum, raisins, and orange zest, followed by the pumpkin and apple, and mix everything together well.

Gently fill the prepared cake pan with the batter and bake in the oven for 10 minutes. Reduce the heat to 340°F and cook for a further 50 minutes, until the cake is lightly golden, the sides are coming away from the inside of the pan, and a skewer inserted into the middle of the cake comes out clean.

Remove the cake from the pan and transfer to a wire rack to cool. Decorate the top of the cake with red currants and dust with confectioners' sugar to serve.

La pastiera

WHEAT & CANDIED FRUIT CAKE

Suor Serena, my favorite nun, has a particular love for *Tosca*. As the opera's protagonist awaits his execution, we hear a melancholy aria: "The stars were shining, the earth was fragrant, the garden gate creaked, and a footstep brushed the sand. She entered, fragrant, and fell into my arms. And I've never loved life as much." To Suor Serena, this song resembles the preparation of *pastiera*: the combination of cooked wheat, eggs, ricotta, and candied fruit is transformed into a declaration of lust for life. Fireworks, confidences, and Puccini in the kitchen.

Preparation time: 25 minutes plus soaking and chilling

Cooking time: 1¼ hours

Makes 1 x 9-inch cake

1½ tablespoons unsalted butter, plus extra for greasing

3½ tablespoons raisins

3 tablespoons milk

7oz canned cooked wheat (available in good Italian delicatessens or online)

rind of 1 lemon, cut into chunks

¾lb ricotta cheese

1½ cups superfine sugar, divided

3 eggs, separated

2 tablespoons orange blossom water

1 teaspoon cinnamon powder

3½ tablespoons candied orange peel, chopped

½ cup chopped walnuts

Pastry:

1 egg

2 cups bread flour, plus extra for dusting

½ superfine sugar

1 teaspoon baking powder

¾ stick unsalted butter

2 tablespoons limoncello liqueur

zest of 1 lemon

Grease and line a 9-inch nonstick springform cake pan with parchment paper.

Place the raisins in a small bowl of water and let soak for 30 minutes, then drain and squeeze them dry with your hands.

Meanwhile, make the pastry. Put the egg, flour, sugar, baking powder, butter, liqueur, and lemon zest into a food processor and mix together to form a dough. Roll into a ball, seal in plastic wrap, and let rest in the refrigerator for 30 minutes.

Preheat the oven to 375°F.

Melt the butter in a saucepan. Add the milk, wheat, and chunks of lemon rind and let simmer over low heat for 10 minutes.

Beat the ricotta together with half the sugar in a bowl. In a second bowl, beat the egg yolks with the remaining sugar until fluffy. In a third bowl, whisk the egg whites together with the orange blossom water and cinnamon until stiff. Using a wooden spoon, gently mix the ingredients from all three bowls together and fold in the candied orange peel, raisins, and walnut pieces.

Unwrap the chilled pastry and cut off two-thirds. Sandwich the larger piece between two sheets of parchment paper and roll it out into an 11½-inch circle. Transfer to the bottom of the prepared cake pan, carefully pushing the pastry 1¼ inches up the sides of the pan. Let chill in the refrigerator for 10 minutes.

Roll out the remaining pastry between sheets of parchment paper as before and cut it into 10 strips measuring 9 x ¾ inches. Arrange the strips on a sheet of lightly floured nonstick parchment paper and let chill in the refrigerator for 5 minutes.

Remove the pastry crust from the refrigerator and pour the wheat cream into it. Gently place the pastry strips on top in a criss-cross lattice pattern and bake for 1 hour, until the strips are slightly browned and a toothpick inserted into the center of the cake comes out clean. Let cool for at least 30 minutes to allow the filling to become firm before serving.

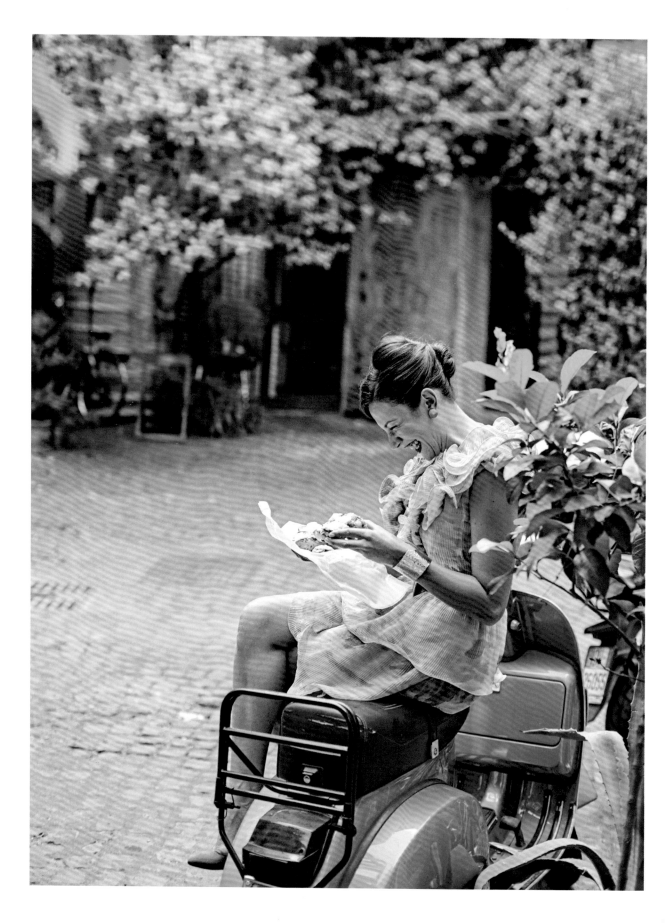

Chapter 3

LUNCH ON THE RUN

When it comes to matters of the stomach, there's no such thing as waiting politely in line in Italy. On any weekday, in an *alimentari* (deli) or a *rosticceria* (rotisserie) tucked away on a side street, you will see hungry men and women, young and old, builders and bankers, pushing in front of each other with no apologies: it's lunchtime warfare. The staff at the *alimentari* will make succulent panini from scratch for customers coming in for a quick lunch between midday and 3 P.M. (yes, that's the length of a typical lunch break in Italy, often followed by a totally deserved siesta. Of course). Usually a long long line forms behind the old lady who has unwittingly managed to get to the *alimentari* just a few minutes before everybody else. She's in no rush and takes her time choosing between a filling of Taleggio or robiola cheese, explaining to the man behind the counter why one is better than the other for her cholesterol, while remarking on the ignorance of her useless doctor, who keeps telling her otherwise. But what does he know? At this point the builder impatiently waiting his turn will probably holler a typical Roman hyperbole: *"A nonna, qua stamo a fa' notte"*—"Hey, grandma, it's getting dark outside!" This is the cue for everyone else in the shop to breathe a loud sigh of relief while nodding vigorously at each other.

And then there's the store assistant who always slices the cured ham too thickly. He will put it on the scales and feigning innocence ask: "It's actually 120 grams. What shall I do? Shall we keep it?" No use reminding him that you had only asked for 80 grams. By this point, the customer will have been waiting in line for more than 15 minutes and is in a hurry, having left his car parked illegally. Chances are you will later see him gesticulating wildly, trying to convince a policeman not to fine him by explaining how he absolutely had no choice but to park in front of two other vehicles on a pedestrian crossing. Talking loudly is considered a sign of affection in Rome. Enjoy these discussions that can stop the traffic of an entire city, where everybody is entitled to their opinion and to make it known. And all that noise only to see, five minutes later, friends and foes bite into a Rosetta con Mortazza (*see* page 69) in total #foodhappiness mood. Go hard or go home.

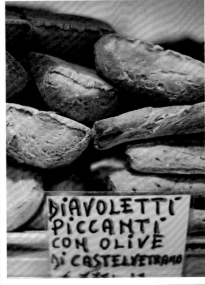

DIAVOLETTI
PICCANTI
CON OLIVE
DI CASTELVETRANO

e la barca va...

RICE-STUFFED TOMATOES WITH POTATOES

This is Roman street food *par excellence*, the sort of thing you would get in a *rosticceria* to take back home or to the office. I like to inject a little fun into the kitchen by taking what was once in vogue and bringing it up to date, and this retro dish is definitely ready for a comeback. I love the way such simple ingredients can turn into something so tasty. Eye-catching red parcels, perfect for a cozy meal in that most exclusive restaurant: your own kitchen.

Preparation time: 30 minutes plus cooling

Cooking time: 2½ hours

Serves 6

2 tablespoons extra virgin olive oil, plus extra for oiling

5½lb russet potatoes, peeled, parboiled in salted water, and cut into chunks

handful of rosemary leaves

3 cloves garlic, peeled and left whole, divided

1¼ cups vegetable stock (*see* page 12)

6 large high-quality tomatoes, each weighing about 7oz

2 tablespoons chopped flat-leaf parsley leaves

2 tablespoons chopped basil leaves

2 tablespoons chopped thyme leaves

1 cup arborio or carnaroli risotto rice

½ cup grated Parmesan cheese

¼ cup grated pecorino romano cheese

2¼oz scamorza, haloumi, or *mozzarella da cucina* (cooking mozzarella), cut into 6 pieces

salt and pepper

Preheat the oven to 350°F. Line two baking pans with nonstick parchment paper.

Lightly oil an oven dish or roasting pan and add the parboiled potato chunks, rosemary, and two garlic cloves. Cover with the stock, transfer to the oven, and cook for 1 hour, or until the potatoes are soft and slightly browned at the edges. Drain the potatoes and set aside to cool.

Meanwhile, prepare the tomatoes. Slice off the top one-third of each tomato and reserve (these will act as the "lids" for the stuffed tomatoes). With a spoon, scoop out the pulp and juices of the tomatoes, transfer them to a food processor, and blend together until smooth. Sprinkle the inside of the tomatoes with salt and set them upside down on a wire rack to drain.

Gently fry the remaining garlic clove in the olive oil until browned, then add the blended tomato and let simmer for 10 minutes over low heat until thickened. Remove the garlic, season to taste, and stir in the chopped herbs. Set aside.

Boil the rice in abundant salted water following the package directions for about 15 to 18 minutes, until *al dente*, then drain and transfer to a bowl with the tomato sauce and grated Parmesan and pecorino cheeses. Stir together well.

Place the tomatoes on one of the prepared baking pans. Fill each with a tablespoon of the rice mixture, add a piece of scamorza, and cover with more rice to fill. Arrange the tomato caps on the other baking pan. Drizzle the tomatoes and lids with oil and season with pepper. Transfer to the oven, placing the tomato lids on the bottom rack, and bake for 55 minutes, turning the broiler up to high for the final 5 minutes of cooking, until golden brown.

Remove the tomatoes and lids from the oven and let cool for 5 minutes. Put the lids on the tomatoes and serve with the potatoes.

Rosetta con mortazza, stracchino e mostarda casalinga

ROSETTA LOAF WITH MORTADELLA, STRACCHINO CHEESE & HOMEMADE MOSTARDA

When I snuck into the oldest *forno* in town for an impromptu lecture on Ancient Roman breadmaking, the baker was surprised by my interest in this loaf. "Rosetta is only for the sentimental retired people, who, to tell you the truth, still make the best panini with it. But it's not fashionable any more. What are you, a gladiator?" A gladiator, me? I'm just acting on common sense: try this soft, airy piece of ecstasy with mortadella, mild, creamy stracchino cheese, and homemade *mostarda* and, before you know it, you'll embrace its timeless charm. Good bread calls for a golden rule: always add salt away from yeast, otherwise your attempt will be doomed from the start. But if you pay attention to a few details, the result will be so scrumptious, therapeutic, and rewarding I assure you you'll want to make it a regular habit.

Preparation time: 35 minutes plus rising and cooling

Cooking time: 1¼ hours

Makes 6 sandwiches

1¼ cups water

2 teaspoons fast-acting dry yeast

4 cups bread flour, plus extra
  for dusting

3 tablespoons extra virgin olive oil

1 teaspoon superfine sugar

2 tablespoons sea salt flakes

10½oz mortadella or ham of
  your choice

9oz stracchino or other soft
  cheese, cut into 6 thick slices

Mostarda **(makes enough to
fill 2 x 9oz jars):**

2 cups water

2 cups superfine sugar

1½lb general-purpose apples,
  peeled, cored, and cut into
  wedges

½ cup white wine vinegar

3 teaspoons English or wholegrain
  mustard

For the *mostarda*, bring the measured water to a boil in a saucepan. Stir in the sugar until fully dissolved, then add the apples and cook over low heat for 35 to 40 minutes, without stirring, until the mixture is sticky and like jam in consistency. Let cool for 30 minutes.

Meanwhile, heat the vinegar in another saucepan over low heat until it is just about to boil. Stir in the mustard, transfer to a small bowl, and let cool for 30 minutes.

Once the apple and vinegar mixtures are cool, fish the apple wedges out of their syrup and set them aside. Add the syrup to the mustardy vinegar and mix well. Pack the apple wedges into two warm, sterilized 9-ounce jars (*see* page 254), add the syrup mixture to cover, seal tightly, and set aside until needed.

Line a baking pan with baking paper and fill a spray bottle with water.

Pour the measured water into a small bowl, add the yeast, and stir to dissolve. Sift the flour, yeast mixture, and oil into a large mixing bowl or the bowl of an electric stand mixer fitted with the dough hook and knead together for 10 minutes to form a dough. Then add the sugar and knead for another 5 minutes. Knead for a final 5 minutes, gradually adding the salt as you go, until the dough is soft and smooth. Transfer the dough to a bowl, cover it with a clean dish cloth, and let stand in a warm place to rise for 1½ hours.

Separate the dough into six equal-sized pieces and roll each into a ball. Place the dough balls on the lined baking pan, leaving ¾ inch between each one.

Dust with a little flour, then, using an apple cutter, gently press down on each dough piece to about halfway in order to give the rolls their distinctive "rosetta" markings. (If you don't have an apple cutter you can use the rim of a coffee mug to make this mark, although it won't give the bread the same distinctive shape). Cover the baking pan with a dish cloth and let stand to prove for a further 45 minutes.

Preheat the oven to 425°F.

When you're ready to bake, dust the proved rolls with a little more flour. Spray the inside of the oven 7 to 8 times with your water bottle, then quickly insert the proved rolls on the baking pan and close the oven door. Bake for 25 to 30 minutes, spraying the inside of the oven every 5 minutes, until the bread is risen and thoroughly cooked and the crust is a deep golden brown. Remove from the oven and transfer to a wire rack to cool.

Cut the rosetta rolls in two horizontally, leaving the pretty rose shape intact. Divide the stracchino and mortadella evenly between the roll bottoms, spoon a little of the *mostarda* over each, and sandwich together with the roll tops to close.

Consume your rosetta within 24 hours, or freeze it to make a stupendous packed lunch in the future. The *mostarda* will keep for up to 6 months, stored in a sealed jar in a dry place away from sunlight.

"Panino" di mozzarella

MOZZARELLA "SANDWICH"

Wherever I may be, when the clock strikes noon, I can feel an almost tangible excitement in the air. So here is what I do: I pour myself a drink, whatever is in the house—usually the wine left over from the previous night—and set out to make some soul-satisfying food. Most of the time, it's little nibbles made with leftovers. That's when those ingredients sitting in the refrigerator looking all gloomy and disoriented come back to life and feel useful at last! This version of a mozzarella panini will transport you directly to a state of happy helplessness.

Preparation time: 10 minutes

Cooking time: 10 minutes

Serves 4

1 garlic clove, peeled and left whole

1 tablespoon extra virgin olive oil, plus extra for drizzling

½ zucchini, thinly sliced

4 x 4½-oz balls buffalo mozzarella, drained

1 large tomato, cut into 4 slices

small handful of basil leaves

salt and pepper

In a skillet, heat the whole garlic clove in the oil over medium heat for 2 to 3 minutes until golden. Remove and discard the garlic clove, add the zucchini to the pan, and cook, stirring, for 10 minutes until the zucchini is soft and lightly browned. Season with salt and transfer to a small bowl.

Cut each mozzarella ball in half. Divide the zucchini and tomato slices between the mozzarella halves, drizzle with oil, and press the halves back together, tucking a basil leaf into each mozzarella "sandwich." Season with salt and pepper to taste.

Conchiglioni ripieni su foglie di basilico

STUFFED CONCHIGLIONI PASTA ON BASIL LEAVES

On weekends, Via del Corso is where young people go to check one another out. They call it *lo struscio*, a casual stroll through the streets of the city, arms wrapped around each other companionably. In this dish, which can be enjoyed either warm or cold, the pasta shells, filled with sauce, evoke memories of this traditional Italian way of spending leisure time. Enjoy the enticing voluptuousness of making the sauce—you can take your time. Any leftover sauce makes a magnificent sandwich filling.

Preparation time: 15 minutes

Cooking time: 15 minutes

Serves 4 as a main

5 baby plum tomatoes

1 avocado

1 tablespoon salted capers, rinsed, divided

1/3 cup extra virgin olive oil, divided

3 anchovy fillets in olive oil

12oz canned tuna in springwater, drained

3/4 cup pitted black olives, very finely chopped

1 celery stalk, trimmed and very finely chopped

1 red onion, very finely chopped

large handful of basil leaves, chopped, plus extra whole leaves to garnish

2 small handfuls of sage leaves, chopped

14oz conchiglioni pasta

1 garlic clove, peeled and left whole

large handful of flat-leaf parsley leaves

2 tablespoons bread crumbs (*see* page 262)

1 tablespoon dried oregano

salt and white pepper

Place the tomatoes in a bowl and add boiling water to cover. Leave for 1 to 2 minutes, then drain, cut a cross at the stem end of each tomato, and peel off the skins. Cut into 1/4-inch cubes.

Halve the avocado, scoop out the flesh with a spoon, and cut into 1/4-inch cubes. Finely chop half the capers.

Heat 1 tablespoon of olive oil together with the anchovy fillets in a large pan over medium heat. Add the tuna, breaking up any large chunks into smaller pieces, and cook, stirring, for 5 minutes. Then stir in the tomato, avocado, chopped capers, olives, celery, onion, basil, sage, and 3 tablespoons of olive oil. Season with a pinch of white pepper and remove from the heat.

Bring a large saucepan of salted water to a boil, add the conchiglioni, and cook following the package directions until *al dente*. Drain the pasta and pass it quickly under cold water to prevent it from cooking further.

In a large pan, gently brown the garlic with the remaining 2 tablespoons of oil. Remove the garlic from the pan, then add the conchiglioni. Stir well to coat the pasta shells in the garlic-scented oil.

Spoon the filling into the conchiglioni. Place in a large dish on a bed of basil leaves, scatter with the chopped parsley, bread crumbs, oregano, and the remaining whole capers, and serve.

Fagottini di verza ripieni

SAVOY CABBAGE VEAL BUNDLES

This recipe is a requiem to a way of life that's now fading away. Exploding with colors, it's an inviting combination of flavors competing for your palate's attention. These tantalizing small cabbage parcels can be served warm or cold—any leftovers can be kept in the refrigerator for up to five days—and are good with a simple green salad, drizzled with balsamic vinegar. Put a considerable portion of these small cabbage parcels in an airtight container and take them to work with you for a tantalizing, flavor-filled lunch.

Preparation time: 20 minutes

Cooking time: 40 minutes

Serves 4

5½oz white cabbage, red cabbage, or chard leaves

10½oz organic ground veal (tenderloin or round)

3½oz mortadella

⅓ cup peanuts, roasted or unsalted

1 teaspoon chopped dill fronds

1 large egg

⅓ cup grated Parmesan cheese

1 teaspoon chopped flat-leaf parsley leaves

1 teaspoon chopped basil leaves

2 tablespoons unsalted butter

1 small white onion, chopped

1¾oz pancetta or smoked bacon cubes

1 garlic clove, peeled and left whole

2 sage leaves

3 tablespoons dry white wine

½ cup vegetable stock

salt and pepper

Bring a large saucepan of salted water to a boil, add the cabbage leaves, and blanch for 5 minutes. Drain and let cool on a clean dish cloth.

Once the cabbage is cool, coarsely chop a handful of the leaves. Put the chopped leaves into a food processor with the veal, mortadella, peanuts, dill, egg, Parmesan, parsley, and basil and blend together to form a coarse paste. Season with salt and pepper.

Take a spoonful or so of the filling and place in the center of a blanched cabbage leaf. Carefully roll the leaf up and secure it with a toothpick. Repeat with the remaining leaves and filling.

Melt the butter in a skillet over medium heat, add the chopped onion, bacon, garlic, and sage and cook for 10 minutes until the onion has softened. Arrange the cabbage rolls in the pan, pour the white wine and stock evenly over them, season with salt, and cook for 25 minutes. When the liquid has reduced to a thick glossy sauce, the bundles are ready.

Carpaccio di spigola con pesche, kiwi e rughetta

SEA BASS CARPACCIO WITH PEACHES, KIWI & ARUGULA

Carpaccio is the most sublime expression of meat or fish. Beware though, for that marvel to happen the main ingredient must be at its freshest. The most important steps of this recipe should be completed by your trusted and scrupulous fish dealer, who will fillet your sea bass, skin it, and then cut it diagonally into very thin slices. From there on in, it's easy. A riotous rainbow of color and pattern that will brighten up even the darkest of days.

Preparation time: 10 minutes plus marinating

Serves 4

1 fennel bulb, leaves reserved to garnish

½ cup freshly squeezed lemon juice

3 tablespoons extra virgin olive oil

pinch of sea salt flakes

1 x 1lb 5oz sea bass, trimmed, filleted, and cut into 1¾oz slices (ask your fish dealer to do this for you)

To garnish:

1¾oz wild arugula

1 ripe white peach, peeled and cut into thin wedges

1 ripe kiwi, peeled and cut into thin slices

2 teaspoons pink peppercorns

Cut the fennel bulb into 6 slices and put into a food processor with the lemon juice, olive oil, and salt. Blend everything together to form a smooth paste.

Cut each fish slice into strips measuring 2 x 1 inches. Arrange the fish pieces in the center of a shallow serving bowl. Strain over the fennel and lemon juice mixture and cover with plastic wrap. Chill in the refrigerator for 30 minutes to marinate.

Once the fish has marinated, remove it from the refrigerator and garnish with the arugula, fennel leaves, fruit pieces, and peppercorns. Serve immediately.

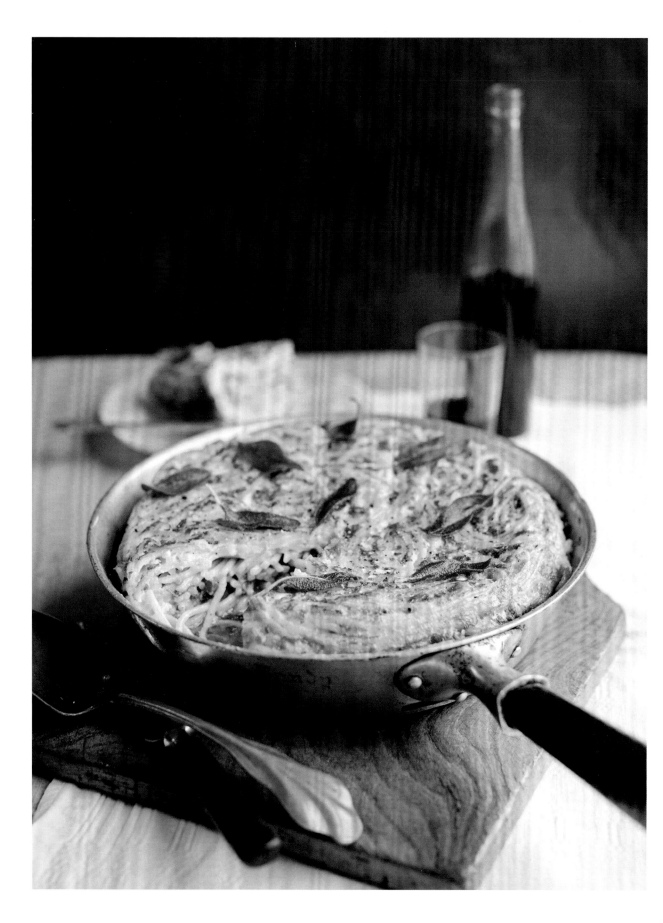

Frittata di spaghetti

SPAGHETTI OMELET

"Qui n'se butta gniente." That's Roman for: "Nothing gets thrown away here." In the old days, lunchtime was marked by placing a huge bowl of *spaghetti al sugo* in the middle of the table, to be eaten greedily by all diners. Any leftovers would be revived in a new shape: the frittata. I must admit, I am so evangelical about the food I like eating (and cooking) that I relish an opportunity to use up ingredients that might otherwise simply be thrown away. The quintessential comfort food snack, *frittata di spaghetti* can also be sandwiched between pieces of bread (try the Rosetta on page 69) for a picnic—the *panino con la frittata* has been a Roman favorite for decades.

Preparation time: 10 minutes

Cooking time: 30 minutes

Serves 6

6 large eggs

1/2 cup grated pecorino romano cheese

1/2 cup whole or skim milk

pinch of salt

pinch of pepper

3 1/2 oz provolone, Muenster, or mozzarella cheese, cut into 1 1/4-inch cubes, divided

14oz spaghetti

3oz pancetta or smoked bacon cubes

1/3 cup extra virgin olive oil, divided

large handful of sage leaves, finely chopped, plus 10 whole sage leaves

Beat the eggs together in a bowl, add the pecorino, milk, salt, pepper, and half the provolone and mix together well. Set aside.

Bring a large saucepan of salted water to a boil, add the spaghetti, and cook following the package directions until *al dente*. Drain the pasta and let it cool for a minute, then tip it back into the pan, add the beaten egg mixture, and mix everything together so the pasta is evenly coated.

Heat a small nonstick skillet over low heat, add the pancetta, and fry for 3 minutes until crisp and golden. (You won't need any oil here—the fat from the pancetta will be sufficient.) Remove the pancetta from the skillet and set aside. Fry the whole sage leaves in the remaining pancetta fat until crisp—about 30 seconds—and set aside.

In a large nonstick skillet, heat 1/4 cup of the extra virgin olive oil over medium heat. Add half the spaghetti to cover the bottom of the pan and scatter it with the chopped sage, pancetta cubes, and remaining provolone, then cover with the rest of the spaghetti. Lower the heat and cook gently for 10 minutes, or until the omelet has just set. Turn the omelet over with the aid of a plate if you need it, add the remaining 2 tablespoons of olive oil, and continue to cook for a further 5 minutes until the omelet is firmly set and golden in parts.

Let the omelet rest in the pan for 10 minutes before turning out and serving, scattered with the fried sage leaves.

Soppressata di polpo con insalata di patate e sedano

OCTOPUS "KEBAB" WITH POTATO & CELERY SALAD

Fishermen used to beat the octopus they'd just caught against a rock to tenderize it, but I suggest you get your fish dealer to do the hard work for you. Freezing your octopus following the method outlined here will also help kickstart the tenderizing process. Once ready, you can slice the octopus thinly to serve it as a carpaccio or turn it into a lunch on the run by cutting it into thicker slices and using it to fill panini. Octopus rules.

Preparation time: 30 minutes plus cooling and freezing

Cooking time: 1 hour 20 minutes

Serves 6

1 small carrot

1 celery stalk, trimmed

1 white onion

1 tomato

2 bay leaves

1 teaspoon white vinegar

10 black peppercorns

3 juniper berries

4 cloves

1/3 cup coarse rock salt

3lb 5oz fresh octopus, eyes and beak removed (ask your fish dealer to do this for you)

2 large round red or round white potatoes, peeled

handful of flat-leaf parsley leaves, finely chopped

handful of dill fronds, finely chopped

1 teaspoon ground nutmeg

2 tablespoons extra virgin olive oil

Dressing:

2 tablespoons extra virgin olive oil

1 teaspoon salt

1 tablespoon pepper

1/4 cup lemon juice

Fill a large saucepan with water, add the carrot, celery, onion, tomato, bay leaves, vinegar, peppercorns, juniper berries, cloves, and salt and bring to a boil.

Carefully lower the octopus briefly into the water until fully submerged, then lift it out of the pan. Repeat this process 9 more times, until the tentacles have curled up and softened, then lower the octopus once more into the water. Cover with a lid, and let simmer gently over very low heat for 50 minutes, then add the potatoes and cook for a further 30 minutes.

Once the cooking time is up, remove the vegetables from the cooking liquid. Finely slice the celery and dice the potatoes into 1/2-inch cubes, put them in a bowl, and let chill in the refrigerator. Let the octopus cool in its cooking liquid for 30 minutes (this will prevent it from getting chewy), then drain and pat dry with paper towels. Cut the octopus into six big chunks, leaving the tentacles intact.

With a sharp knife, cut off the tapered end of an empty 52 fluid ounce plastic bottle and pierce the bottom a few times using a pair of scissors or the tip of a sharp knife. Resting the bottle in the sink, insert the octopus and let the excess water drain through the holes you've made at the bottom of the bottle. Using something heavy like a meat tenderizer or a pestle, push the octopus as far down into the bottle as it can go, then cover with plastic wrap and place a can of beans or tomatoes on top to act as a weight. Place in the freezer for at least 10 hours.

When ready to serve, remove the octopus bottle from the freezer, turn the bottle upside down, and let the octopus slide out. Using a sharp knife, cut the octopus "kebab" into either thin or thick slices, according to your taste.

For the dressing, mix together the ingredients in a small bowl until well combined. Drizzle the octopus slices with the dressing.

Arrange the potatoes and celery in a serving dish and top with the dressed octopus slices. Scatter with the parsley and dill, sprinkle with the nutmeg, and drizzle with olive oil.

EGGPLANT & ZUCCHINI "BOATS"

This recipe, with its elaborate simplicity, is like a witty conversation that touches the heart with exquisite common sense and deadpan humor but doesn't take long to get to the point with a matter-of-fact flair. An enticing, all-year-round vegetable dish.

Preparation time: 20 minutes, plus resting

Cooking time: 1 hour 20 minutes

Serves 4 as a main

Eggplant "boats":

2 large eggplant (about ¾lb each), trimmed and cut in half

1 tablespoon extra virgin olive oil, plus extra for oiling

4 salted anchovies, rinsed and chopped

½ cup pitted black olives, chopped

1 teaspoon chopped flat-leaf parsley leaves

¾ cup bread crumbs (*see* page 262)

1 garlic clove, sliced

1 teaspoon dried oregano

¼ cup salted capers, rinsed

⅔ cup cherry tomatoes, halved

salt and pepper

Zucchini "boats":

4 large zucchini

7oz roast ham, finely chopped

5½oz provolone or scamorza cheese, finely chopped

1 teaspoon ground nutmeg

pinch of dried red chili flakes

1 tablespoon extra virgin olive oil

5½oz sharp Cheddar cheese

For the eggplant "boats," score the flesh of each eggplant half with a sharp knife in a criss-cross pattern, sprinkle with 2 tablespoons of salt, and let rest skin-side down on a wire rack for 1 hour to extract any bitter juices. Rinse and dry the eggplant halves with paper towels or a clean dish cloth.

Preheat the oven to 340°F. Lightly oil two baking dishes.

Mix the chopped anchovies, olives, and parsley together in a bowl. Add the bread crumbs and stir in the garlic, oregano, and capers. Season with salt and pepper and mix together well.

Arrange the eggplant halves in one of the prepared baking dishes, divide the tomato halves equally between them, and spoon over the bread-crumb mixture. Drizzle with the oil and bake in the oven for 1 hour until the bread-crumb mixture is golden and the eggplant are soft and tender. Remove from the oven and set aside.

For the zucchini "boats," bring a large saucepan of salted water to a boil. Add the whole zucchini and boil for 5 minutes, then drain and let cool.

Increase the heat to 400°F.

When the zucchini are cool enough to handle, trim the ends and cut in half. Using a spoon, gently scoop the softer flesh from the middle, strain it to remove any excess water, and put it in a bowl along with the chopped ham, provolone, nutmeg, chili flakes, and olive oil. Season with salt and mix everything together well.

Spoon the stuffing into the hollowed-out zucchini halves and place them in the second prepared baking dish. Top each "boat" with a fine grating of Cheddar cheese and bake in the oven for 10 minutes until the cheese has melted and the filling is golden. Serve alongside the zucchini either warm or cold, accompanied by an equally healthy green salad.

Gnocchi alla ricotta del giovedì con gamberetti e pistacchi

THURSDAY'S RICOTTA GNOCCHI WITH SHRIMP & PISTACHIOS

A few years ago, I realized that my job as a journalist didn't allow me to do justice to all the tiny details of life that fascinated me. That was when I started to live and breathe through the redemptive power of food. Just like my career path, preparing gnocchi is a slow-building process. Historically, it made sense for Roman Catholics to eat something filling on Thursday, the day before they were forbidden to eat meat. *Ridi, ridi, che mamma ha fatto i gnocchi.* Keep smiling, all is well, mommy made you gnocchi.

Preparation time: 30 minutes plus cooling

Cooking time: 25 minutes

Serves 6

3lb 5oz russet potatoes, peeled and cut into ½-inch chunks

3¾ cups all-purpose flour, plus extra for dusting

3½oz ricotta cheese

1 large egg

salt

Sauce:

¼ cup extra virgin olive oil

1 garlic clove, peeled and left whole

1lb 2oz cooked, shelled jumbo shrimp

1¼ cups unsalted pistachios, crushed to a fine powder, divided

3 tablespoons unsalted butter, cut into ½-inch cubes

Bring a large saucepan of salted water to a boil, add the potato chunks, and cook over medium heat for 10 to 15 minutes, until the potato pieces are completely cooked through but not so soft that they are falling apart. Drain and set aside until cool enough to handle, then mash them with a potato masher or fork until smooth. Season with salt to taste and set aside to cool.

For the sauce, heat the oil in a large skillet over low heat, add the garlic clove, and cook gently until golden to infuse its flavor into the hot oil. Remove the garlic, add the shrimp to the pan along with half the crushed pistachios, and cook for 5 minutes until the shrimp are just lightly golden but not overcooked. Remove the pan from the heat, add the butter, and stir to melt into the hot shrimp. Set aside.

In a large bowl, mix the flour, ricotta, and egg together with the mashed-potato mixture using your hands until everything comes together to form a soft, yellow dough. Tip the dough out onto a lightly floured work surface and knead for 2 to 3 minutes until firm, then divide into quarters. Roll each piece of dough into a cylinder approximately 1¼ inches thick and divide each into ¾-inch pieces. Lightly press down on each gnocchi with the tines of a fork to give them their typical curly shape and dust with a little more flour.

Bring a large saucepan of salted water to a boil. Place a serving bowl by the side of the stove and fill it with half the sauce along with a ladleful of the boiling salted water.

Add the gnocchi to the pan and poach for 2 to 3 minutes, or until they float up to the surface of the water. As the gnocchi come to the surface, scoop them up with a slotted spoon and place them in the bowl with the sauce. Spoon the remaining sauce over the gnocchi and fold gently to mix well, then sprinkle with the rest of the crushed pistachios to finish. Serve outrageously hot.

Ceci e baccalà

FRIDAY'S SALT COD WITH CHICKPEAS

Some like it hot. I like it not. This dish is divine served cold on the day of the week when Romans traditionally renounce meat to offer patronage to the best fish in town. When preparing this dish, I go for convenience. Italian cooking is not that complicated, really. It just takes time. For this recipe, you would usually use salt cod, which needs to be soaked for about 24 hours, but I'd rather go with the fresh version, which is less salty and more tender. The cooking method is *al guazzetto*, that is to say, is in a very fluid wine sauce.

Preparation time: 10 minutes

Cooking time: 15 to 20 minutes

Serves 4

2/3 cup vegetable stock

1/3 cup extra virgin olive oil, divided

1 garlic clove, peeled and left whole

2 rosemary sprigs, leaves picked

1 teaspoon ground cumin

handful of sage leaves

2 x 9-oz cans cooked chickpeas in water, drained

1lb 5oz cod, haddock, or monkfish fillets

1/2 cup all-purpose flour

1 teaspoon salt

large handful of kaffir lime leaves

1/2 cup dry white wine

Gently warm the stock in a saucepan.

Heat half the oil in a skillet over medium heat. Add the garlic clove, rosemary leaves, cumin, and sage leaves and fry gently for 2 to 3 minutes until the garlic is browned. Remove and discard the garlic, add the chickpeas, season with salt, and cook for 5 to 10 minutes, or until they have softened and are beginning to break up. Pour the contents of the pan into a food processor and blend together, gradually adding the warm stock, until the mixture has a consistency like purée. Return to the pan and keep warm.

Drain and rinse the fish well, then cut it into 1/2-inch cubes. Put the flour and salt in a bowl, add the fish cubes, and toss to coat evenly.

Heat the remaining oil in a large skillet. Wrap each fish cube in a lime leaf, securing it in place with a toothpick. Transfer the mini fish parcels to the pan and cook for 1 minute on each side, then add the wine and bring to a vigorous simmer. Cook for 5 minutes until the wine has evaporated, then remove from the heat and serve with the chickpea purée.

Chapter 4 FAMILY LUNCHES

On Sundays, the world stops in Rome. The streets fall quiet at lunchtime. The busiest places around midday are either churches or *pasticcerie*, where Romans buy *pastarelle* (*see* page 30) for their families—having been instructed not to dare come home empty-handed—while inside the houses, everyone's attention is focused on the kitchen. The youngest child is often entrusted with the fundamental task of verifying that the pasta is cooked *al dente*, while the older kids set the table. Over lunch, the mother will gently (or not so gently) slap the arms of the little ones to remind them of their table manners—"Don't slouch!", "Get your elbows off the table!"—while the nonno will make a toast to celebrate the day of rest, with his glass filled half with red wine and half with water.

At *il pranzo della domenica*, superstitions passed down from generation to generation are still observed. For example, having 13 people around a table is considered akin to inviting bad luck. Should you accidentally find yourself with 13 for lunch, you can always have the children sit at a separate table. No children in the family? Just set an extra place with an empty chair. Spilling salt on the tablecloth or pretty much anywhere else is also inauspicious. Should that happen, you must throw a pinch of salt over your left shoulder with your right hand. Spilling wine, however, brings good luck, so much so that each diner must immediately dip a finger in the spilled wine and dab the back of their ears in order to share in the inevitable good fortune that will surely follow. These gestures are all part of a mosaic, a form of magical interpretation of reality, and the following chapter is both a walk down memory lane and a vivid look at modernity.

In order to demonstrate a respectable measure of conviviality, every Italian table will have at least one loaf of bread on it. After overindulging in Sunday's Pasticcio di Cappelletti (*see* page 114) or ornamental Vitel Tonné (*see* page 118), most of us opt for a *scarpetta*: we take a piece of bread and mop up the delicious leftover sauce on our plate. It'd be bad manners and bad luck not to. Beware of all imitations.

Gnocchi alla Romana con sugo di spuntature di maiale

ROMAN-STYLE SEMOLINA GNOCCHI WITH PORK RIB SAUCE

In Ancient Rome people didn't believe that creativity came from human beings. They gave credit to a heavenly spirit that came from some otherworldly place: *il Genio*. This spirit would subtly reveal itself to the artist, guiding him or her. My beloved readers, just like those artists I need divine intervention to protect myself from overtesting this recipe. Not an easy task, since these pork ribs are a delectably juicy pleasure, which could very well be out of this world.

Preparation time: 30 minutes plus cooling

Cooking time: 2½ hours

Serves 6

4⅓ cups milk

1 stick unsalted butter, divided, plus extra for greasing

2 teaspoons ground nutmeg

2 juniper berries, crushed

1½ cups semolina

2 egg yolks, beaten

1½ cups grated Parmesan cheese, divided

salt

Sauce:

⅓ cup extra virgin olive oil

1 large white onion, coarsely chopped

1 celery stalk, trimmed and coarsely chopped

1 carrot, coarsely chopped

1lb 5oz pork ribs

1lb 5oz pork sausages

4 cups passata (sieved tomatoes)

2 cloves

handful of thyme leaves, chopped

pinch of red chili flakes (optional)

salt

For the sauce, heat the oil in a large saucepan over low heat, add the onion, celery, and carrot and cook gently, stirring occasionally, for 15 minutes, until softened and golden.

Remove the vegetables from the pan and set aside. Add the pork ribs and sausages and brown well on all sides, then pour in the passata and ½ cup of water. Return the vegetables to the pan, bring to a gentle simmer, and cook over low heat, covered, for 1 hour. Season with salt, stir in the cloves, thyme, and red chili flakes, if using, and cook for a further hour, until the sauce has thickened and reduced. Remove from the heat and set aside.

For the semolina gnocchi, heat the milk together with a walnut-sized lump of butter, the nutmeg, juniper berries, and a generous pinch of salt in a large saucepan. Bring to a boil, then gradually sift in the semolina, stirring vigorously with a whisk to prevent any lumps from forming. Cook over low heat for 3 minutes, until the semolina is thick enough that a spoon can stand up in the mixture, then remove the pan from the heat and let cool slightly for 10 minutes.

Preheat the oven to 350°F. Grease one 13 x 9-inch baking dish and a second 9 x 9-inch baking dish with a little butter.

Once the semolina mixture has cooled, stir in the egg yolks and half the grated Parmesan. Pour the mixture into the large prepared baking dish to a layer of about ½ inch. Wet your hands and press your palms on the semolina to level it off. Let cool for a further 15 minutes.

Using the rim of a wine glass, cut out as many disks as the amount of semolina allows. Arrange the disks in the regular baking dish, overlapping them slightly, and sprinkle with the remaining Parmesan. Melt the remaining butter and drizzle it over the semolina gnocchi.

Bake the gnocchi for 25 to 30 minutes, until golden. Warm the tomato sauce and serve with the gnocchi.

*Coda di rospo agli agrumi e finocchio accompagnata da fagiolini corallo
in salsa di noci, melograno e mango*

CITRUSY MONKFISH WITH FENNEL ACCOMPANIED BY RUNNER BEANS IN A WALNUT, MANGO & POMEGRANATE DRESSING

With its bright citrus flavors, this is honest, straightforward, uplifting food. In Rome, runner beans are called *fagioli corallo* or coral beans, probably because they look as if they might grow underwater. In trattorias, you will find them floating in tomato sauce. This side dish proves that in the kitchen, as in life, there's something more important than logic: imagination. In the US, runner beans are also known as "Kentucky Wonder" pole beans, an Heirloom variety.

Preparation time: 15 minutes

Cooking time: 25 minutes

Serves 6

3/4 cup all-purpose flour

6 monkfish fillets, cut into 1/2-inch cubes

1/4 cup extra virgin olive oil

1/2 stick unsalted butter

2 fennel bulbs, cut into 1/2-inch chunks and fronds reserved

1/2 cup water

1/4 cup lemon juice

2 teaspoons fennel seeds

salt and white pepper

Runner beans:

1 garlic clove, peeled and left whole

1lb 5oz runner beans, trimmed

1oz chives, finely snipped

8 walnuts, shelled

1 tablespoon grated Parmesan cheese

2 tablespoons white wine vinegar

1/4 cup extra virgin olive oil

1/4 large mango, peeled and diced

1/2 cup pomegranate seeds

salt and pepper

For the runner beans, half-fill a large pan with water, add the garlic clove, and bring to a boil. Add the beans to the pan with a little salt and cook for 5 minutes or until tender, then drain well under cold water, reserving 3 tablespoons of the garlicky cooking water. Set aside.

Mix the chives, walnuts, Parmesan, vinegar, olive oil, mango, pomegranate seeds, and reserved cooking water together in a small bowl. Season with salt and pepper to taste and set aside.

Put the flour in a large food bag together with the monkfish pieces, seal securely, and shake to coat the fish.

Gently heat the oil and butter together in a large Dutch oven. Add the fennel chunks and measured water, increase the heat to medium, and let simmer for 10 minutes, then stir in the coated fish pieces, lemon juice, and fennel seeds. Season with salt and white pepper to taste.

Cook for a further 10 minutes, turning the fish pieces over occasionally to ensure they are evenly cooked. Scatter with the fennel fronds and serve immediately with the lemon slices and alongside the beans, drizzling them with the dressing before serving.

Spiedini di manzo ripieni con tortino di agretti

FILLED BEEF ROLLS WITH AGRETTI TART

In Rome, if you look closely, reminders of the past are everywhere. In a city that is already the epitome of vintage, you'll find shops selling all kinds of memorabilia, like posters for Italian neorealist movies, depicting postwar Rome as if suspended in time, radiating monumental grandeur and unattainable virtues.

For me, this stupendously colorful dish—the perfect excuse to use up any odds and ends you have lurking in the refrigerator—encapsulates the sense of nostalgia that permeates the city. When shopping for this recipe, look for radicchio with crisp leaves, with no signs of wilting or browning. This dish also features agretti (also known as friar's beard), a grasslike Italian green with a delicately mineral taste, though you can use samphire instead should agretti prove difficult to find.

Preparation time: 15 minutes

Cooking time: 1 hour 25 minutes

Serves 6

$^{1}/_{3}$ cup extra virgin olive oil, divided, plus extra for brushing

2 large red onions, 1 finely sliced, 1 cut into quarters and separated into petals

$5^{1}/_{2}$oz Belgian endive, trimmed and finely sliced

$1^{1}/_{2}$ cups bread crumbs, divided (*see* page 262)

1lb 2oz beef fillet, cut into $^{1}/_{4}$-inch slices

$5^{1}/_{2}$oz prosciutto or roast ham, coarsely chopped

$5^{1}/_{2}$oz Fontina, provolone, Bel Paese cheese, coarsely chopped

24 bay leaves

Tortino di agretti:

1 tablespoon extra virgin olive oil

1 small red onion

7oz agretti (friar's beard) or samphire

Place six bamboo skewers in a bowl, cover them with water, and let them soak (this will prevent them from burning later during cooking).

Heat 3 tablespoons of olive oil in a nonstick skillet over medium heat, add the sliced red onion, and cook for 5 minutes until golden. Remove and set aside half the onion, add the Belgian endive, reduce the heat to low, and cook for a further 15 minutes, until the endive has softened and is tender.

Tip the endive mixture into a food processor and blend together with $^{1}/_{2}$ cup of the bread crumbs to form a smooth paste.

Using a rolling pin, flatten the beef slices on a clean work surface until they measure approximately 4 inches in diameter. Cut each slice in two. Place a tablespoon of the endive mixture and a teaspoon each of the chopped prosciutto and cheese in the center of each beef piece and wrap everything up like a parcel. Repeat with the remaining beef pieces until all the ingredients are used.

Alternately thread the meat parcels, bay leaves, and onion petals onto the soaked bamboo skewers, allowing four meat parcels per skewer. Brush the skewers with a little oil and coat with the remaining bread crumbs. Set aside.

For the *tortino*, heat the oil in a nonstick skillet over low heat, add the onion (reserving a few slices to finish the dish) and a pinch of salt, and cook for 5 minutes, or until the onion has started to soften. Increase the heat to medium, add the agretti and three-quarters of the radicchio, cover, and cook for a further 10 minutes until the leaves have wilted and are soft. Remove the lid and cook for a further 1 to 2 minutes, then season with salt and pepper and set aside.

Preheat the oven to 350°F. Lightly butter a $6^{1}/_{4}$-inch round cake pan. Alternatively, to make individual servings, lightly butter 6 ramekins or

10¹/₂oz Trevisano radicchio bulbs
  or red Belgian endive heads,
  trimmed and cut into strips,
  divided
unsalted butter, for greasing
10¹/₂oz ricotta cheese
¹/₂ cup grated Parmesan cheese
1 egg, plus 2 egg whites
salt and pepper

To garnish:
drizzle of balsamic vinegar
1²/₃ cups croutons

6 holes of a muffin pan. Using the bottom of a ramekin or muffin cup as a guide, cut out 6 circles of parchment paper and place one in the bottom of each ramekin or muffin cup.

Beat the ricotta in a bowl with a wooden spoon until creamy and fluffy, then stir in the cooked vegetables, Parmesan, egg, and egg whites. Season generously with salt and pepper and mix together well.

Place the cake pan on a roasting pan with high sides. Pour the filling into the pan, then pour boiling water into the roasting pan up to two-thirds of the pan's depth. Carefully transfer to the oven and bake for about 45 to 50 minutes (or 20 to 25 minutes if using ramekins or a muffin pan), until the *tortino* is set and lightly golden. Remove from the oven and let cool.

While the *tortino* is cooling, cook the *spiedini*. Heat the remaining 2 tablespoons of olive oil in a nonstick skillet, add the skewers, and brown them gently for 3 minutes on each side until shiny and golden.

Arrange the *spiedini* on a platter. Cut the *tortino* into wedges and garnish with the croutons, a drizzle of balsamic vinegar, and the reserved radicchio and sliced onion. Serve.

Pasta al forno con asparagi, pancetta e provola

BAKED PASTA WITH ASPARAGUS, PANCETTA & PROVOLA CHEESE

Meals with friends and family call for comfort food, and the addition of asparagus turns baked pasta into a feast. This recipe is just as mouthwatering when eaten cold, making a yummy treat for a refrigerator raider like me. Topped with pancetta, this dish is an overwhelming embrace of the senses. Tall or short, wise or fool, believe me, no one can resist it.

Preparation time: 20 minutes

Cooking time: 1 hour

Serves 6

1lb 2oz asparagus or wild asparagus

2 tablespoons extra virgin olive oil

1 leek, trimmed, cleaned, and finely sliced

1 stick unsalted butter, plus extra for greasing

2 cups milk

1 teaspoon ground nutmeg

3/4 cup all-purpose flour

14oz fusilli or penne pasta

5 1/2 oz provolone, Fontina or medium Cheddar cheese, divided

5 1/2 oz pancetta or smoked bacon cubes

1/2 cup bread crumbs (*see* page 262)

salt

Prepare the asparagus by breaking off and discarding the woody ends, cutting off and reserving the tips and slicing the stalks into 1/2-inch chunks.

Put the asparagus tips into a small saucepan of boiling salted water and blanch for 3 minutes. Drain and set aside.

Bring a second saucepan of salted water to a boil, lower to a gentle simmer, and keep to one side.

Heat the olive oil in a nonstick skillet, add the leek, and cook, stirring, for 5 minutes until browned. Add the asparagus stalks, season with salt, and cook for 20 minutes, stirring occasionally and adding a ladleful of hot water every 5 minutes to prevent everything from sticking to the bottom of the pan, until the asparagus stalks are soft and cooked through. Tip the asparagus and leek mixture into a food processor and blend together well. Set aside.

Preheat the oven to 350°F. Grease a 14 x 8-inch baking dish with a little butter.

Gently heat the milk in a small saucepan, ensuring it doesn't boil. In a separate saucepan, melt the butter, add the nutmeg and flour, and stir together to make a smooth paste (roux). Season with salt and slowly add the warm milk, stirring constantly, to form a smooth, creamy sauce. Bring to a gentle boil, then remove from the heat and set aside.

Bring a large saucepan of salted water to a boil, add the pasta, and cook for half the cooking time indicated on the package, or about 3 to 7 minutes. Drain and place in a bowl along with the sauce, two-thirds of the provolone, and half the blended asparagus. Mix everything together well and pour into the prepared baking dish.

Scatter with the asparagus tips and pancetta cubes, pour over the remaining asparagus mixture, and shred the remaining provolone evenly over the top. Transfer to the oven and bake for 20 to 25 minutes, or until the surface has formed a nice golden crust.

Sprinkle with the bread crumbs and cut into rectangles. Serve hot or cold.

Filetto di salmone con mousse di fave e pecorino

SALMON FILLET
WITH FAVA BEAN & PECORINO MOUSSE

It's May 1st, also known as Workers' Day. From this date on, a string of public holidays and long weekends signal the beginning of summer and its seemingly endless sweet idleness. It's picnic time, and families will arrive in the meadows of the Castelli Romani with baskets filled with bottles of red wine, fresh fava beans, and crystalline pecorino. As the popular proverb says, *"Al cuor non si comanda"* ("you can't rule the heart"). It wants what it wants. Still, how about some pink salmon with minty fava bean mousse as a variation on the theme? Sit down. Tuck that napkin in your collar. Get ready to have your taste buds driven insane.

Preparation time: 10 minutes

Cooking time: 10 minutes

Serves 2

1²/₃ cups fava beans or edamame, defrosted if frozen

2 tablespoons lemon juice

1oz mint leaves, plus extra to garnish

1³/₄oz pecorino romano cheese

¹/₄ cup extra virgin olive oil

walnut-sized lump of salted butter

2 x 9¹/₂oz salmon fillets

salt

Bring a saucepan of salted water to a boil, add the fava beans, and cook for 5 minutes. Drain and skin the beans, then put them in a food processor with the lemon juice, mint leaves, pecorino, and olive oil. Season with salt and blend together briefly for 5 seconds to form a coarsely chopped "mousse."

Melt the butter in a skillet over low heat, add the salmon fillets, and cook for 3 to 5 minutes on each side until lightly golden.

Transfer the salmon fillets to individual plates and spread the fava bean mousse over the surface of each. Scatter with a few extra mint leaves and enjoy with a full-flavored white wine, such as Greco di Tufo.

Pasta alla carbonara

PASTA WITH CARBONARA SAUCE

For centuries, atoning for their sins by paying for the construction and decoration of churches was the standard way of life for Roman nobility. Caravaggio got in on the act, befriending the rich families of his day, and inside the Basilica di Sant'Agostino hangs his *Madonna di Loreto*. Caravaggio used his friends as models, and his Mary is sensuous and real. He also illuminated the scene in a way that proved revolutionary. Let there be light, then.
We find the same shining light in *pasta alla carbonara*, the apotheosis of the Roman kitchen, which owes its name to the charcoal burners (*carbonari*) who used to leave for work with some handy ingredients from which to make lunch. They might have let some coal dust slip in, hence the black peppery finish.

Preparation time: 5 minutes plus chilling

Cooking time: 20 minutes

Serves 4

20 black peppercorns

5 egg yolks, plus 1 egg white

2 cups grated pecorino romano cheese

a sprinkle of ground nutmeg

7oz pancetta cubes

14oz spaghetti

salt

Toast the peppercorns in a small skillet over very low heat for 1 to 2 minutes until fragrant, then grind or crush them to a coarse powder using a mortar and pestle, a meat tenderizer, or the flat side of the blade of a heavy knife.

Transfer the grated pecorino cheese to a food processor and whiz briefly—you want the pecorino to be as finely grated as possible.

In a bowl, whisk together the egg yolks and white for 2 to 3 minutes until pale and creamy. Add two-thirds of the pecorino and mix together well, until glossy and thick. Sprinkle with the nutmeg and a little of the crushed pepper, transfer to the refrigerator, and let chill for 20 minutes.

Fry the pancetta in a small skillet over medium heat, stirring, for 10 minutes until lightly golden (you won't need any oil for this, because the pancetta will release a lot of fat while cooking). Spoon off and discard half the fat from the pan and set the pancetta and remaining fat aside.

Bring a large saucepan of salted water to a boil, add the spaghetti, and cook following the package directions until *al dente*. Drain the pasta, reserving a cupful of the cooking water, and return to the pan.

Pour the chilled egg and cheese mixture over the pasta, then add the crispy pancetta and fat. Quickly stir everything together, adding a splash or two of the reserved cooking water, until the sauce is smooth and creamy. Sprinkle with the rest of the cheese and pepper and serve immediately.

Spezzatino in umido con parmigiana di carciofi

BEEF STEW WITH ARTICHOKE PARMIGIANA

Braised in excellent olive oil, with the meat allowed to steep in its own juices until it is done, this beef stew is like a good marriage: the whole is greater than the sum of its parts. You can enjoy this *spezzatino* either *in bianco*—with white sauce, as suggested here—or *in rosso*, by adding 3 tablespoons of tomato paste for a red sauce. And to simply call artichoke parmigiana a side dish is to underestimate this sumptuous treat. In fact, together, these two dishes make for a perfect gastronomical marriage.

Preparation time: 10 minutes

Cooking time: 2 hours

Serves 8

$2/3$ cup all-purpose flour

3lb 5 oz beefsteak, cut into 2-inch chunks

walnut-sized lump of unsalted butter

$2^1/2$oz pancetta cubes

1 small carrot, very finely chopped

1 celery stalk, trimmed and very finely chopped

1 shallot, very finely chopped

1 garlic clove, peeled and left whole

$1/4$ cup extra virgin olive oil

$2/3$ cup red wine

2 cups beef stock

2 teaspoons dried rosemary

handful of sage leaves

1 bay leaf, plus extra to garnish

salt and pepper

Artichoke parmigiana:

walnut-sized lump of unsalted butter

1 garlic clove, peeled and left whole

1 large white onion, very finely chopped

1 cup passata (sieved tomatoes)

$1/4$ cup dry white wine

Place the flour in a plastic food bag, add the beef pieces, seal the bag securely, and shake to coat.

Melt the butter in a large saucepan over medium heat. Add the pancetta, carrot, celery, shallot, and garlic and cook, stirring, for 5 minutes or until lightly browned. Stir in the oil and wine. Cook for a further 2 to 3 minutes, then add the coated beef pieces. Cook, stirring, for another 2 to 3 minutes until the beef pieces are browned on all sides, then pour in the stock and bring to a boil. Add the rosemary, sage, and bay leaf, and reduce the heat to a simmer. Cover the saucepan and let cook for 1 hour 20 minutes. Uncover and simmer for another 30 minutes, or until the beef is tender and the sauce has thickened and reduced. (If the sauce is still quite liquid at this point, increase the heat and cook for a little longer until it's reduced to the desired consistency). Season with salt and pepper.

While the beef is cooking, make the artichoke parmigiana. Melt the butter in a saucepan over low heat, add the garlic and onion, and cook gently, stirring occasionally, for 5 minutes until golden. Increase the heat to medium, then add the passata, wine, nutmeg, basil, and mint. Simmer gently for 20 to 25 minutes until the sauce has thickened and reduced. Season with salt and set aside.

Beat the beer, flour, and egg together in a small bowl to form a batter.

Drain the prepared artichoke quarters and cut them lengthwise into $1/2$-inch slices. Place the slices between two clean dish cloths to dry.

Pour the vegetable oil into a large heavy saucepan over high heat. When the oil is almost smoking, dip the artichoke slices in the batter, carefully lower them into the hot oil, and fry for 3 minutes until lightly golden (you may need to do this in batches so as not to overcrowd the pan). Remove the artichoke slices with a slotted spoon and drain on paper towels.

Preheat the oven to 350°F.

Smear the bottom of a baking dish with $1/4$ cup of the tomato sauce. Layer the artichokes on top of the sauce, followed by a layer of the cheese slices.

1 teaspoon ground nutmeg

handful of basil leaves, chopped,
   plus extra to serve

handful of mint leaves, chopped,
   plus extra to serve

2/3 cup beer

1/2 cup all-purpose flour

1 egg

8 globe artichokes, cleaned (see
   page 13), quartered lengthwise,
   and placed in acidulated water

1 cup vegetable oil

7oz provolone, scamorza,
   mozzarella da cucina (cooking
   mozzarella) or medium Cheddar
   cheese, cut into 1/2-inch slices

1 1/2 cups grated Parmesan cheese,
   divided

salt

Scatter with a little of the grated Parmesan and some of the remaining basil and mint. Continue to layer in this manner until all the ingredients have been used up, finishing with a last layer of tomato sauce. Bake for 30 minutes until the tomato sauce is bubbling and the surface has slightly browned. Scatter some bay leaves on top to garnish.

Let the parmigiana rest for 10 minutes, then scatter with a few extra mint and basil leaves before serving alongside the stew.

Pesce spada al cartoccio con polpo e scarola in padella

SWORDFISH EN PAPILLOTE WITH OCTOPUS & SAUTÉED LETTUCE

I really admire people who can neatly bone a fish. It definitely does not come easily to me. As the fish is carried to the table, my inner monologue begins: "Will you be kind to me? Oh, don't be such a rascal, people are watching." That's why I often like to cook fish *en papillote*—it is so tender that even the clumsiest eater will be won over. I like to accompany it with baby octopus (if you buy it fresh, freeze it for at least a day before using), luscious crispy morsels cooked in the oven to spare your kitchen the smell of deep-frying. As for the *scarola*, the marriage of salty capers and sweet golden raisins is what makes this lettuce dish so delicious. The flavors are going to send you to the moon and back. Totally worth the journey.

Preparation time: 15 minutes

Cooking time: 30 minutes

Serves 6

$1/2$ cup all-purpose flour

$10^{1}/_{2}$oz baby octopus, cleaned and coarsely chopped

6 swordfish steaks, cut into chunks

$1/3$ cup extra virgin olive oil, divided

$1/4$ cup dry white wine

3 tablespoons chopped thyme leaves

salt and white pepper

Scarola in padella:

$1^{1}/_{2}$ tablespoons extra virgin olive oil

3 garlic cloves, peeled and left whole

$1/3$ cup raisins

$1/3$ cup pine nuts

8 anchovies in olive oil

$1/3$ cup Kalamata olives, pitted

3 tablespoons salted capers, rinsed

$2^{1}/_{4}$lb scarola (prickly lettuce) or escarole, trimmed and leaves separated

Preheat the oven to 400°F.

Put the flour and baby octopus pieces in a large food bag with a few generous pinches of salt. Seal the bag securely and shake well to coat.

Season the swordfish pieces generously with salt and white pepper and brush with 2 tablespoons of the oil. Place a large rectangle of parchment paper in a large baking pan and pour the wine over it. Arrange the swordfish pieces in the center of the paper and scatter with the thyme. Then wrap the paper up to form a loose parcel.

Take a second large rectangle of parchment paper and brush it with 1 tablespoon of oil. Place it next to the swordfish parcel in the baking pan and spread the octopus pieces over it. Drizzle them with the remaining oil.

Transfer the dish to the oven and cook for 15 minutes. Remove the swordfish parcel from the oven and let rest while you return the octopus to the oven to cook for a further 15 minutes until lightly golden and crispy around the edges.

Meanwhile, prepare the *scarola*. Warm the olive oil in a large nonstick skillet over medium heat, add the garlic cloves, and cook for 3 minutes until brown. Remove the garlic from the pan and add the raisins, pine nuts, anchovies, olives, and capers. Cook, stirring continuously, for 2 to 3 minutes until the anchovies have almost dissolved, then add the lettuce, cover the pan, and let cook gently for 15 minutes, or until the lettuce has wilted and turned a glossy green.

Carefully unwrap the swordfish parcel and transfer the fish pieces to a serving dish. Top with the crispy octopus and serve alongside the lettuce.

Pasticcio di cappelletti panna, prosciutto, fegatini e piselli

CAPPELLETTI PASTA CAKE WITH CREAM, HAM, LIVER & PEAS

In Rome's elite gentleman's club, Circolo della Caccia, princes and marquises discuss the profitability of their lands without ever mentioning the "m" word (money) over dinner. The idea of waiters handing individual plated servings to diners is unthinkable here. To bring a serving dish brimming with fragrant delights to the table signifies abundance and conviviality, and waiters gracefully distribute their gastronomic sculptures. Speaking of which, it was once a source of pride for Roman nobility to commission Bernini to chisel their main course. *Pasticcio* is a baroque dish, and I take delight in carving flowers for this luxuriant pasta cake.

Preparation time: 30 minutes plus soaking

Cooking time: 50 minutes

Serves 8 as a main

1oz dried porcini mushrooms (ceps)

1/4 cup extra virgin olive oil

7oz leeks, trimmed, cleaned, and sliced

5 1/2oz chicken livers, trimmed, and chopped

1 2/3 cups frozen garden peas

5 1/2oz roast ham, cut into 1/4-inch strips

1 teaspoon ground nutmeg

1lb 5oz prosciutto cappelletti, Bolognese tortellini or cheese and smoked ham tortellini

1 3/4 cups heavy cream

2 cups grated Parmesan cheese

unsalted butter, for greasing

11 1/2oz ready-made shortcrust pastry sheets, thawed if frozen

1 large egg yolk, beaten

salt and pepper

Put the dried porcini into a small bowl and cover with 1/2 cup of warm water. Let soak for 10 minutes.

Heat the oil in a large skillet over low heat. Add the leeks and chicken livers and cook, stirring, for 5 minutes. Add the peas, ham, nutmeg, and the mushrooms and their soaking water. Simmer gently for 15 minutes.

Bring a large saucepan of salted water to a boil, add the cappelletti, and cook for 1 minute, or until they float to the surface. Quickly drain the pasta and tip it into the saucepan with the leek mixture, adding the cream and Parmesan as you go. Season with salt and pepper to taste.

Preheat the oven to 375°F. Grease a 10-inch pie plate with a little butter.

Roll out the pastry sheets and use one to line the prepared pie plate, cutting off the excess pastry but leaving an overhang of 1 1/4 inches around the edges. Press along the sides to ensure the pastry adheres well, then fill the pastry with the cappelletti and sauce. Cover with the second sheet of dough. Cut off the excess pastry, fold in the overhanging edges, and press with your fingertips to close.

Use the remaining pastry to cut out whatever decorative shapes you would like to adorn your pie.

Brush the surface of the pie with the egg yolk and bake in the oven for 30 minutes until the pastry is golden. Let cool for 10 to 15 minutes before serving with a simple green salad.

Polpette della Nonna accompagnate da scalogni glassati
con prugne secche

GRANDMA'S MEATBALLS
WITH GLAZED SHALLOTS & PRUNES

This is one of the first things I ever learned to make, a scrumptious people-pleaser of a dish—my grandmother's meatballs. There is something dangerously addictive about these mouthwatering morsels, handmade with agile grace. Just try to believe, until #foodhappiness kicks in. If you buy your meat from a butcher, ask for the meat to be ground twice. If not, I suggest you use a sharp knife to grind it again yourself, just as you would when chopping herbs.

Preparation time: 25 minutes

Cooking time: 45 minutes

Serves 6

9oz ground pork

9oz ground beef sirloin

2 eggs

3$^{1}/_{2}$oz Parmesan cheese

handful of flat-leaf parsley leaves, finely chopped

3 tablespoons milk

$^{1}/_{2}$ cup extra virgin olive oil, divided

1$^{1}/_{2}$ cups bread crumbs (*see* page 262)

1 garlic clove, peeled and left whole

1 cup dry white wine

salt and pepper

Glazed shallots and prunes:

$^{1}/_{2}$ stick unsalted butter

3 tablespoons extra virgin olive oil

30 banana shallots, peeled

2 tablespoons liquid honey

$^{1}/_{2}$ cup vegetable stock, plus extra if necessary

30 soft pitted prunes, soaked in warm water for 5 minutes, drained and finely chopped

small handful of sage leaves, chopped, plus extra to garnish

For the glazed shallots, gently heat the butter and oil in a large nonstick skillet, add the shallots, and cook for 1 minute. Then stir in the honey and let cook over very low heat for 30 minutes, occasionally adding a ladleful of stock so that the honey doesn't burn.

While the shallots are cooking, make the meatballs. In a bowl, mix together the ground meats with the eggs, Parmesan, parsley, milk, 2 tablespoons of the extra virgin olive oil, half the bread crumbs, and a pinch each of salt and pepper.

Place the remaining bread crumbs on a large plate. Take a small handful of the meatball mixture and roll it into a walnut-sized ball, then coat it with bread crumbs and transfer to a clean dish. Repeat with the remaining meatball mixture. This recipe makes about 40 small meatballs.

Heat the remaining oil in a large heavy skillet over medium heat. Add the garlic and cook until browned, then carefully place the meatballs in the pan and cook for 2 to 3 minutes per side until golden brown all over. Remove from the heat and transfer the meatballs to a plate covered with paper towels to drain off any excess oil.

Pour the wine into the pan and bring to a vigorous simmer over high heat. Return the meatballs to the pan and cook for a further 5 minutes until the alcohol has evaporated and the sauce has thickened and reduced to a wonderful golden cream.

To finish the shallots, increase the heat to high, add the prunes and sage, and cook, stirring, for 5 minutes until everything has reduced and caramelized.

Serve the meatballs warm or cold alongside the glazed shallots, scattering them with a little extra chopped sage to finish.

Vitel tonné

TUNA-SAUCED VEAL

The origins of this dish are lost in the mists of time. I like to enjoy it cold, with its luscious sauce spread abundantly on top and adorned with glittering capers. I also like to serve it with puntarelle salad (*see* page 120)

Preparation time: 20 minutes plus chilling

Cooking time: 1 hour 30 minutes

Serves 6

3 tablespoons extra virgin olive oil

1 x 1lb 5oz organic boneless veal topside

1 celery stalk, trimmed

1 carrot, peeled

2 garlic cloves, peeled and left whole

1 large onion, peeled

5 bay leaves

small handful of thyme sprigs

1 rosemary sprig

4 cloves

15 black peppercorns

2 cups dry white wine

2 cups vegetable stock

2 teaspoons salted capers, rinsed, plus extra to garnish

Tuna sauce:

3 hard-boiled eggs, peeled

3½oz canned tuna in olive oil, drained

1 teaspoon salted capers, rinsed

6 anchovy fillets

1 tablespoon lemon juice

3 tablespoons extra virgin olive oil

1 tablespoon balsamic vinegar

salt and pepper

Gently heat the olive oil in a large saucepan over low heat. Lower in the veal together with the vegetables, herbs, and spices, pour in the white wine and stock, and bring to a gentle simmer. Cover and cook over low heat for 45 minutes, then remove the lid and cook for a further 45 minutes, until the meat is cooked through and the liquid has reduced by two-thirds.

Once the veal is cooked, carefully remove it from the pan, reserving the cooking liquid, and let cool. Once cool, transfer the veal to the refrigerator and let chill further for at least 20 minutes (this will firm the meat up and make it easier to slice).

While the veal is chilling, make the tuna sauce. Put all the ingredients except the balsamic vinegar in a food processor and season with salt and pepper to taste. Blend until well combined, then, with the motor running, very gradually add the balsamic vinegar and a little of the veal cooking liquid to form a smooth, thick sauce.

Cut the chilled veal into thin slices, arrange on a serving plate, and spoon over the tuna sauce. Top with the capers and serve cold.

Insalata di puntarelle

PUNTARELLE SALAD

Puntarelle is a famously crisp and bitter Roman variant of chicory. It is difficult to get hold of outside of Italy but ask in Italian supermarkets because some growers in California are now producing it. This salad is topped with bocconcini—bite-sized mozzarella—and the leaves are dressed with a glorious anchovy sauce (see photograph on page 119). Bitter is better.

Preparation time: 15 minutes plus cooling

Serves 6

1 puntarelle (winter chicory) head

4 anchovies in olive oil or
    4 teaspoons anchovy paste

1 garlic clove, peeled and left whole

1 tablespoon white wine vinegar

3 tablespoons extra virgin olive oil

1/4 cup lemon juice

10 1/2 oz bocconcini

salt and pepper

Cut off and discard the puntarelle base. Cut the leaves in half lengthwise and then into thin strips before plunging them into a large bowl of iced water. Let stand for 1 hour (this will get the leaves nice and crisp and remove some of their bitterness), then pat dry and set aside in a large bowl.

For the dressing, blend the anchovies, garlic, vinegar, oil, and lemon juice together in a food processor until well combined and season with salt and pepper to taste.

To finish, mix the puntarelle together with the dressing and scatter with the bocconcini.

Cannelloni al forno con ricotta e zafferano

RICOTTA & SAFFRON CANNELLONI

Gabriele d'Annunzio described the inebriating pleasures of Rome: his most famous novel, *Il Piacere*, published in 1889 and known in English as *The Child of Pleasure*, depicts Roman youth in all its pulsating eccentricities. The same capriciousness is to be found in the city's brilliant architectural bric-a-brac. Rome is a multilayered city, one element on top of and inside another. Similarly, these cannelloni hold a secret: the translucent ricotta is hidden under a pasta camouflage and its creamy softness adorns the crispy edges.

Preparation time: 30 minutes plus cooling and resting

Cooking time: 50 minutes

Serves 6

$1/4$ cup extra virgin olive oil, divided

1 red onion, chopped, divided

$1^{1/4}$ cups passata

4 sage leaves

2 red endive heads, trimmed and leaves chopped

$10^{1/2}$oz ricotta cheese

salt and pepper

Pasta:

$2^{1/3}$ cups super-fine grade 00 pasta flour

pinch of salt

3 eggs

Topping:

$1/2$ stick unsalted butter, softened

$3/4$ cup all-purpose flour

4 cups milk

1 teaspoon ground nutmeg

$1/4$ teaspoon saffron threads

$1/2$ cup bread crumbs (*see* page 262)

$1/2$ cup grated Parmesan cheese

salt and pepper

For the topping, melt the butter in a medium saucepan, then remove from the heat and whisk in the flour to form a paste (roux). Whisking all the while to prevent any lumps from forming, gradually add the milk, return the pan to the heat, and continue to whisk until the sauce has thickened to the consistency of custard and is gently bubbling. Stir in the nutmeg and saffron, season generously with salt and pepper, and set aside for at least 30 minutes to cool.

While the topping is cooling, make the pasta. Pile the flour and salt onto a large wooden cutting board or into a bowl, make a well in the center, and crack in the eggs. Beat the eggs lightly with a fork then, using your hands, mix everything together well to form a coarse dough. Knead the dough together until all the pieces have combined and you have formed a velvety smooth lump of dough. (If the dough is looking a little dry, add a few drops of water. If it's too wet, add a little extra flour.) Place the dough in the refrigerator for at least 30 minutes to rest.

Once rested, divide the dough into 12 equal-sized pieces. Roll each out with a rolling pin on a lightly floured surface to a 3 x 6-inch rectangle. Cover with a clean damp dish towel to prevent the pasta from drying out and set aside.

Preheat the oven to 350°F.

For the sauce and filling, place two saucepans over medium heat, adding 2 tablespoons of olive oil and half of the chopped red onion to each. Cook the onion, stirring, for 2 to 3 minutes until slightly softened, then add the passata and sage leaves to one pan and the chopped red endive to the other. Season both pans with salt and pepper and cook, stirring, for 15 minutes, until the tomato sauce has thickened and reduced slightly and the endive has softened.

Remove both pans from the heat, tip the endive into a food processor with the ricotta and blend together well. Set aside. Spoon the passata mixture into a large baking dish.

Bring a large saucepan of salted water to a boil. Working in batches, carefully lower the pasta rectangles into the water and cook for 60 seconds, then transfer to a bowl of iced water to prevent them from overcooking (be careful as you go because the cannelloni are delicate and will tear easily).

Remove the pasta rectangles from the iced water, pat dry with paper towels, and arrange on a clean work surface. Place a tablespoon of filling along the long edge of a pasta rectangle, then roll up gently to create a tubular shape. Carefully place the cannelloni in the prepared baking dish with the open edges down. Repeat with the remaining pasta rectangles.

Spoon the topping over the cannelloni and sprinkle with the bread crumbs and Parmesan to finish. Bake in the oven for 25 minutes, or until the topping is golden and bubbling, then let cool for 10 minutes before serving.

Coda alla vaccinara in verde

GREEN OXTAIL STEW

Feasting is a universal impulse: it's a way of celebrating your community and your taste buds. Throughout history feasts have also been used to display wealth and power. In the 1st century the Roman Emperor Vitellius amazed his guests by serving ingredients gathered from all corners of the Roman Empire, from dormouse livers to peacock brains. This daring but palatable feast boosted trade across the empire. Variety meats have never gone out of fashion in the Eternal City. With its deliciously melting consistency, this oxtail is fit for an emperor.

Preparation time: 10 minutes

Cooking time: 2½ hours

Serves 6

2¼lb oxtail, cut into 6 slices

1 carrot

2 shallots, 1 peeled and left whole, 1 finely chopped

handful each of basil leaves, sage leaves, and mint leaves, chopped, divided

¼ cup extra virgin olive oil

1¾oz *lardo* (*see* page 158), cut into ½-inch cubes

1 garlic clove, peeled and lightly crushed with the side of a knife

½ cup dry white wine

1¾oz baking chocolate, grated

1 celery stalk, trimmed

Celery pesto:

3½oz celery leaves

⅓ cup pine nuts

1 garlic clove, peeled and lightly crushed with the side of a knife

½ cup grated Parmesan cheese

½ cup grated grated pecorino romano cheese

½ cup extra virgin olive oil

Bring a large saucepan of salted water to a boil. Add the oxtail slices, carrot, whole peeled shallot, and half the chopped herb leaves. Let simmer for 1 hour, then carefully remove the meat with a slotted spoon and set aside, reserving the stock.

Gently heat the olive oil in a large saucepan with the *lardo*. Add the chopped shallot and crushed garlic clove and cook, stirring, for 5 minutes or until the garlic starts to brown.

Remove the garlic clove, add the oxtail slices, and cook, stirring, for 2 to 3 minutes to mix everything together well. Season with salt and pepper, pour in the wine, and bring to a simmer, then cover and cook over medium heat for 45 minutes, stirring occasionally and adding a ladleful of stock whenever necessary to prevent the meat from drying out. Add the celery stalk and continue to cook for 45 minutes, stirring, until the oxtail meat begins to fall off of the bones.

While the oxtail is braising, make the pesto. Put the celery leaves, pine nuts, garlic, and grated cheeses in a food processor and blend together briefly. Add the olive oil and a ladleful of the reserved stock and blend together again to form a smooth paste. Set aside in a small bowl.

Once the oxtail is cooked, remove the meat from the bones, and transfer it to a serving dish (the celery and shallot mixture can be set aside and used as stock for tomorrow's risotto). Spoon the celery pesto onto the oxtail, scatter with the remaining chopped herb leaves, and sprinkle with the grated baking chocolate to finish.

Biancomangiare

WHITE SOUP

This dish dates back to the Middle Ages and takes its name from the fact that it consists only of white ingredients. In the Roman Catholic world, the color white symbolized purity. Most of the churches in Rome are made of white marble, whereas the color schemes of people's houses go from the light beige of aristocratic palazzos to the earthy orange of the houses inhabited by artisans of all sorts, from the *pizzicagnolo* (specialist grocer) to the shoemaker. Nutritious and slightly sweet, this is a soup traditionally recommended for new mothers and convalescents—Roman food in its oldest and purest form.

Preparation time: 10 minutes

Cooking time: 35 minutes

Serves 4

1½ quarts water

1 carrot, peeled

1 large tomato

1 large white onion, peeled

1 potato

1 celery stalk

7oz chicken breast fillet

7oz stale sourdough bread

⅔ cup milk

2 teaspoons salted butter

1¾ cups trimmed and halved
    raw white mushrooms

1 cup ground almonds

1¾oz fresh ginger root,
    peeled and grated

7oz croutons

1 cup grated Parmesan cheese

sea salt flakes and pepper

Bring the measured water to a boil in a large saucepan with the carrot, tomato, onion, potato, and celery. Add the chicken breast and a small handful of sea salt flakes and poach gently for 20 minutes, then carefully remove the meat with a slotted spoon, place it on a clean dish cloth, and set another dish cloth on top of it to dry the chicken off. Discard the vegetables and set the stock aside.

Place the bread in a large serving bowl, cover with the milk, and let soak.

Melt a little butter in a skillet over medium heat, add the mushrooms, and sauté for 10 minutes until softened and lightly golden.

Remove the mushrooms from the pan and let cool, then coarsely chop them together with the chicken breast and mix them with the stale bread, almonds, and ginger to form a creamy mush. Transfer to a blender and blitz until smooth.

Return the stock to a boil.

When ready to serve, add a ladleful of the boiling stock to the bowl containing the chicken mixture to yield a consistency like soup. Scatter with the croutons, then pour in the remaining stock. Stir everything together well, season with salt and pepper, sprinkle with the Parmesan cheese, and serve.

Chapter 5 APERITIVO

The working day is finally over. Everybody is out in the streets, enjoying the last rays of the incredible orange Roman sun that has the power to light up all buildings, cupolas, and hearts. The scent of incense and flowers pervades the air, while artisans and *gelatai* alike yawn the end of the day away. What started off at the beginning of the afternoon as an innocent daydream and a vague desire to chill out with your friends after work has now swiftly turned into a vital need for a drink. In Rome, it's time for the *aperitivo*.

A relatively new social phenomenon, the *aperitivo* is characterized by booze, food that is easy on the mouth, and plenty of good conversation. It usually starts after working hours and can last until 9p.m., or all night long, depending on the temperature outside and the number of people who have assembled to chat, discuss, and argue the evening away. It's also just another way to consume a light dinner. Most respectable bars will have a counter dedicated to all things edible designed to accompany a tantalizing drink, usually including arancini, Tramezzini (*see* page 146), rice salads, *crocchette* (*see* page 134), cheeses, *supplì* (*see* page 134), Panzanella (*see* page 132), Alici Marinate (*see* page 147), and anything else that might put a smile on the eater's face.

Behind the Piazza Navona in Rome, there's a bar called Bar del Fico. Old folks with expressive bristly mustaches and unshakeable optimism, who still live in this historic neighborhood, gather to play chess under the trees that decorate a tiny square. You can see them concentrating on the game, surrounded by a crowd made up of people of all ages with a Negroni (*see* page 268) in one hand and a cigarette lighter in the other, talking in raspy voices, almost seeming to grate out the words. I'm inclined to think that it must have taken a lot of cigarettes, smoked in an exceptionally heartfelt style, together with the strategic Roman art of being actively lazy, to produce these particular voices. They're keen to predict the next move in the game of chess, all overjoyed astonishment and amiable severity, while also talking about the latest blockbuster movie or "deciding on" their soccer team's lineup for the next game. It's not just all about women and cars.

MOZZARELLA IN A CARRIAGE

Rome is the title of a brief and enchanting unfinished work by the 19th-century Russian novelist Nikolai Gogol. He talks of how carriages were filled with people of all classes during Carnival season, their faces covered with flour and beaming with joy, for once mixing with one another—for the rest of the year, the division would be rather more brutal. In this recipe, the "carriage" is filled with cheese. Use fully drained *mozzarella da cucina*, the most basic cooking mozzarella, which you can find in any supermarket—it's also the cheese to use for your *pizzette* (*see* page 55).

Preparation time: 5 minutes

Cooking time: 5 minutes

Serves 6

12 white or brown bread slices, crusts removed and cut into quarters

5^1/$_2$oz *mozzarella da cucina* (cooking mozzarella), cut into ^{1}/$_8$-inch slices

1 x 3^1/$_2$-oz jar of anchovy fillets in olive oil, drained

small handful of rosemary leaves

^{1}/$_2$ cup milk

^{3}/$_4$ cup all-purpose flour

2 eggs

^{1}/$_2$ cup vegetable oil

Arrange the bread quarters on a large plate or a clean work surface. Place a slice of mozzarella, 1 anchovy fillet, and a few rosemary leaves on half of the bread quarters, then use the remaining bread quarters to sandwich together.

Pour the milk into one shallow bowl and the flour into another. Beat the eggs and add them to a third bowl.

Take the sandwiches, one by one, and dunk them first into the milk, then dredge them in the flour, then dip them in the beaten egg.

Heat the oil in a large skillet over medium heat, carefully add the sandwiches, and cook for about 1 minute on each side until crisp and golden (you may have to do this in batches depending on the size of your pan). Drain briefly on paper towels and serve immediately.

Panzanella

BREAD SALAD

In the mild midsummer evenings, I walk around the narrow streets of this splendid city, my ears pricked for the ever-present sound of a mandolin. I'm right at home as I walk past the Pantheon through Piazza della Rotonda, which truly feels like a large living room to me. Who needs to visit art galleries when you have an open-air museum at your feet? I like to make myself this salad and have an impromptu picnic sitting on a marble bench, never bored with having my breath taken away. Improvisation—that's how I do summer.

Preparation time: 10 minutes plus resting

Cooking time: 5 minutes

Serves 4

¼ cup extra virgin olive oil, divided

7oz rustic bread loaf, torn into bite-sized pieces

4 firm tomatoes

2 large red onions, peeled

1 cucumber, cut into ¾-inch cubes

1 celery stalk, trimmed and cut into ¾-inch cubes

15 pitted black olives, finely chopped

1½oz arugula leaves, finely chopped

small handful of basil leaves, finely chopped

1 tablespoon white or red wine vinegar

3½oz pecorino romano cheese, cut into ¾-inch cubes

salt and pepper

Heat 2 tablespoons of olive oil in a large nonstick skillet over high heat. Add the bread pieces and fry, turning occasionally, for 5 minutes until crisp and golden all over. Remove from the heat and set aside.

Place the tomatoes in a bowl and add boiling water to cover. Let stand for 1 to 2 minutes, then drain, cut a cross at the stem end of each tomato, and peel off the skins. Cut the tomatoes approximately into ¼-inch cubes, discarding the seeds.

Slice the onions and place them in a bowl of cold water for 10 minutes. Drain and dry on a clean dish cloth.

In a salad bowl, mix together the sliced onions, chopped cucumbers, celery, tomatoes, and olives, then add the chopped arugula and basil leaves, pour in the vinegar and the remaining 2 tablespoons of oil, and season with salt and pepper. Finish the panzanella by adding the toasted bread pieces and giving everything a final gentle stir to ensure the bread is covered in all the juices. This salad is delicious served immediately, or you can keep it in the refrigerator for up to 3 days, letting it absorb the mixture of aromatic flavors. Scatter with the pecorino before serving.

FRITTER TRIO OF ROMAN-STYLE RICE BALLS, POTATO CROQUETTES & MINI MEAT LOAVES

Bernini and Borromini shared between them the most desirable sculptural and architectural commissions to be carried out in Rome in the 17th century, yet rumor has it they were fierce enemies. On Piazza Navona, you'll see Borromini's Church of Sant'Agnese in Agone. Facing it is Bernini's fountain of the Four Rivers. Allegedly, Bernini designed two of the fountain's four allegorical figures to make fun of his rival: one with his hand raised to protect himself from the building's imminent collapse, and the other with his head hidden under a veil in disgust. Sacred and profane, history and legend—in other words, *fritto misto all'italiana*.

Preparation time: 50 minutes plus chilling

Cooking time: 1¼ hours

Serves 4

5 eggs, beaten

4 cups bread crumbs
(*see* page 262)

½ cup all-purpose flour

1¾ cups vegetable oil

Supplì:

2 tablespoons extra virgin olive oil

1 x 10½-oz veal brain, cleaned
and chopped

1 cup passata (sieved tomatoes)

½ cup red wine

small handful of flat-leaf parsley
leaves, chopped

2 cups beef stock

½ stick unsalted butter, divided

1 small white onion, chopped

2 cups risotto rice

1 cup grated Parmesan cheese

1 egg, beaten

7oz Fontina cheese, cut
into 1¼-inch strips

For the potato croquettes, put the mashed potatoes in a bowl together with the thyme, Parmesan, and the beaten egg and mix together well. Transfer to the refrigerator to cool.

For the *supplì*, warm the oil over low heat in a medium Dutch oven. Add the veal brain and cook, stirring, for 10 minutes until the brain pieces are almost melted, then add the passata and wine. Increase the heat to medium and cook for a further 30 minutes, adding the parsley halfway through cooking, until the sauce has thickened and reduced.

Warm the beef stock in a saucepan. Melt half the butter in a medium saucepan, add the onion, and fry for 5 minutes until softened. Add the rice, increase the heat to high, and cook, stirring, for 2 to 3 minutes until the rice is translucent. Lower the heat and keep stirring while adding the warm stock gradually, allowing each ladleful to be absorbed before adding the next, for 12 to 15 minutes or until the rice is plump and tender. Remove the rice from the heat and add the Parmesan, beaten egg, and remaining butter and stir gently to combine. Stir in the tomato sauce and season with salt and pepper, then spoon the mixture into a large serving dish. Transfer to the refrigerator to chill and become firm.

For the meat loaves, bring a large saucepan of salted water to a boil. Add the onion, celery, carrot, beef, and chicken, reduce to a simmer, and cook for 1 hour over low heat. Lift the meat out of the stock with a slotted spoon and let cool, then tip it into into a food processor with the soaked bread, garlic, mortadella, Parmesan, parsley, lemon zest, rosemary, nutmeg, and beaten egg. Blend together well, then stir in the mashed potatoes and season with salt and pepper. Using your hands, shape the mixture into 1½-inch balls, then pat each with your palm to form flattened loaves.

Potato croquettes:

1¾lb russet potatoes, baked until tender then mashed

small handful of thyme leaves

1¼ cups grated Parmesan cheese

1 large egg, beaten

2¼oz *mozzarella da cucina* (cooking mozzarella), cut into 1¼-inch strips

2¼oz roast ham, cut into 1¼-inch strips

salt and pepper

Meat loaves:

1 small onion, peeled

1 celery stalk, trimmed

1 small carrot, peeled

5½oz beef

5½oz chicken breast, cut into chunks

3½oz stale bread, soaked in ½ cup milk

1 garlic clove, peeled and left whole

1¾oz mortadella

½ cup grated Parmesan cheese

handful of flat-leaf parsley leaves, chopped

zest of 1 lemon

1 teaspoon dried rosemary

1 teaspoon ground nutmeg

1 large egg, beaten

1 x 7-oz russet potato, baked until tender then mashed

salt

Now form the *supplì* and potato croquettes. For the *supplì*, take a strip of Fontina, form a little ball of rice around it, and squeeze it into a sausage shape. Repeat with the remaining cheese and rice. For the croquettes, take a piece of mozzarella and a piece of ham, form a little ball of mashed potatoes around it, and squeeze it into a sausage shape. Repeat with the remaining cheese, ham, and potatoes.

Pour the beaten eggs, bread crumbs, and flour into three separate bowls. Dip the potato croquettes and meat loaves in the flour, then into the beaten egg, and finally into the bread crumbs to coat evenly. Dip the *supplì* in the eggs and then into the bread crumbs.

Heat the oil in a large heavy saucepan or deep-fryer until it reaches 350 to 375°F or a cube of bread dropped in the oil browns in 30 seconds. Carefully add the *supplì*, croquettes, and meat loaves in batches and cook for 1 to 2 minutes on each side until golden brown all over. Remove from the oil with a slotted spoon and drain on paper towels. Serve warm and tantalizingly crisp.

Olive all'ascolana

ASCOLI-STYLE STUFFED OLIVES

In Rome, blue cars mean a special category of people, who can use dedicated routes and park wherever they like. These blue cars should be a privilege of government elites, but it doesn't take long to realize that the person you saw jumping a red light was not an important politician, but the friend of a cousin of the Minister's secretary. Nunzio, the barman, tells me: "*Bella signorina*, it's all about who you know." As I understand it, once you know "the right people," you can go a long way in Rome, at least without ever having to take a bus . . . These round, golden morsels are so good they must be illegal somewhere, but surely not around here. Nepotism, a glass of bubbly, and stuffed olives.

Preparation time: 20 minutes plus chilling

Cooking time: 30 minutes

Serves 4

2 tablespoons extra virgin olive oil

1 small carrot, finely chopped

1 small onion, finely chopped

1³/₄oz pancetta or smoked bacon, finely chopped

1 celery stalk, trimmed and finely chopped

¹/₄lb ground beef

¹/₄lb ground pork

¹/₄lb ground chicken

¹/₂ cup dry white wine

²/₃ cup vegetable stock

zest of ¹/₂ lemon

²/₃ cup grated Parmesan cheese

1 teaspoon ground nutmeg

1 garlic clove, peeled

2 eggs, divided

1¹/₂ cups bread crumbs (*see* page 262), divided

60 large green olives, pitted

¹/₂ cup all-purpose flour

1¹/₄ cups vegetable oil

salt

Heat the oil over low heat in a large skillet, add the carrot, onion, pancetta, and celery and cook, stirring, for 5 minutes, until the vegetables have softened. Add the ground meats and cook gently, stirring occasionally, for 10 minutes, until browned all over. Then add the wine and stock, bring to a vigorous simmer, and cook for a further 10 minutes, or until the liquids have evaporated.

Remove the pan from the heat and transfer the contents to a food processor. Add the lemon zest, Parmesan, nutmeg, clove, one of the eggs, and one-third of the bread crumbs. Mix everything together to form a smooth, soft paste. Season with salt to taste.

Spoon the filling into a pastry bag with a small tip attached and squeeze the filling into the olives.

Arrange the flour in one shallow bowl and the remaining bread crumbs in another. Beat the remaining egg and tip it into a third shallow bowl. Roll the stuffed olives first in flour, then in the egg, and then in the bread crumbs. Transfer the olives to the refrigerator to chill for 20 minutes, then repeat the dipping process to ensure a thorough coating.

Heat the vegetable oil in a large heavy saucepan or deep-fryer until it reaches 350 to 375°F or a cube of bread dropped in the oil browns in 30 seconds. Carefully add the olives and cook for 1 to 2 minutes per side until golden brown all over. Remove from the oil with a slotted spoon and drain on paper towels. Serve warm.

Fiori di zucca ripieni

STUFFED ZUCCHINI FLOWERS

For as long as I can remember zucchini flowers have been one the main protagonists of the Roman food scene. Yes, their pistils and stamens need to be meticulously removed before you can eat them, but don't be discouraged. Beyond their apparently hard-to-handle appearance, these delectable blossoms are soft yet crunchy, perfectly suited for frying as well as for making a delicious pizza topping. In this recipe they are stuffed with a mixture of glorious cheeses. Accompany the stuffed flowers with a glass of Chianti for a perfect little appetizer.

Preparation time: 15 minutes

Cooking time: 5 minutes

Serves 4

extra virgin olive oil, for greasing

12 large zucchini flowers

9oz ricotta cheese

3^1/$_2$oz Taleggio, Fontina, or other semisoft cheese

1 teaspoon ground nutmeg

1 teaspoon white pepper

3 tablespoons grated Parmesan cheese, divided

^{1}/$_2$ cup bread crumbs (*see* page 262)

salt

Preheat the oven to 350°F. Lightly oil a large baking pan.

Using a sharp knife, cut off any bumpy growths around the base of each zucchini flower and trim away the majority of the stem, leaving about ^{1}/$_2$ inch attached (this will not only help keep the flowers together but will also look pretty). Gently cut open the zucchini flowers lengthwise, being careful not to break them, and remove the stamens or pistils. Alternatively, instead of cutting open the flowers, gently peel apart the petals, being careful not to tear them.

In a bowl, mix together the ricotta, Taleggio, nutmeg, and white pepper with half the Parmesan and season with salt.

Using either a pastry bag or a teaspoon, carefully fill the zucchini flowers with the cheese mixture. Close the flowers, twisting the ends of the petals to seal, then transfer to the prepared baking pan. Scatter with the bread crumbs and the remaining Parmesan and bake in the oven for 5 minutes until the zucchini flowers are lightly golden. Serve warm.

Galantina di pollo servita con bocconcini d'uva al formaggio

CHICKEN GALANTINE WITH CHEESE-DIPPED GRAPES

Preparation time: 30 minutes plus marinating and chilling

Cooking time: 2 hours 25 minutes

Serves 8

3½oz veal topside, cut into ½-inch chunks

7oz pork loin, cut into ½-inch chunks

3½oz mortadella

3½oz prosciutto

2 cups Marsala wine

3 quarts water

1 carrot

1 celery stalk, trimmed

1 tomato

1 potato

1 large white onion, studded with 6 cloves

1 egg

large handful of dried porcini mushrooms (ceps)

1 x 3¼-lb freerange chicken boned

1⅔ cups unsalted pistachios, coarsely chopped

4 black summer truffles, coarsely chopped

sea salt flakes

Cheese-dipped grapes:

1¼ cups unsalted pistachios, coarsely chopped

3½oz Gorgonzola cheese

½ cup cream cheese

small bunch of seedless white grapes

One of the world's first cookbooks, compiled in the 4th century and named *Apicius* after a Roman gourmet, includes a recipe for stuffed chicken, a dish prepared for superb banquets. This recipe for chicken galantine is a little elaborate but you will be so pleased with the result. The whole process of tying up the chicken and simmering it in stock is rather reminiscent of a time gone by that we should try to hold on to. Tradition in evolution. Try it to believe it.

Place the veal and pork pieces together with the mortadella and prosciutto in a large bowl, pour in the Marsala, and let marinate for 30 minutes.

Meanwhile, bring the measured water to a boil in a large saucepan with the carrot, celery, tomato, potato, and clove-studded onion. Add a small handful of sea salt flakes, reduce the heat, and simmer gently, covered, for 25 minutes.

Remove the meat pieces from the marinade and transfer to a food processor along with the egg, porcini mushrooms, and a pinch of salt. Blend everything together to grind the meat and form a thick, creamy paste.

Lay the chicken on a cutting board skin-side down and spread the creamy meat mixture over the top. Scatter with the pistachios and truffles and roll up into a fat log, tucking in the ends as you roll. Place on a clean dish cloth and roll up tightly, then tie the chicken in three or four places with kitchen string to help it keep its shape and ensure even cooking, trimming off any extra string around your knots.

Immerse the chicken in the stock, cover with a lid, and let simmer over low heat for 2 hours.

While the chicken is simmering, make the cheese-dipped grapes. Put the chopped pistachios in a bowl. In a second bowl, mix both cheeses together with a whisk until light and creamy. Dip the grapes, still on their stems, first into the cheese mixture and then into the pistachios to coat evenly. Transfer to the refrigerator to chill.

Once the galantine is ready, remove it from the stock and transfer it to the refrigerator for at least 4 hours to chill and set (alternatively you could place it in the freezer for 1½ hours if you're in a hurry; just don't forget it's there!).

When ready to serve, remove the strings from the chicken and carve it into thin slices. Arrange on a serving dish and garnish with the cheese-dipped grapes.

Sandwich di polenta con salsiccia e formaggio

POLENTA SANDWICH
WITH BAKED SAUSAGE & CHEESE

I'm going slightly off track here with polenta, a staple of northern Italy. Originally made in huge portions, this golden cornmeal porridge was then spread out on wooden slabs and topped with sausage. *La morte sua*—to die for. It's still considered a *cibo povero* today (a pocket- as well as a crowd-pleaser) and you can now find little polenta snacks during the *aperitivo* hour in Rome.

Preparation time: 20 minutes plus cooling

Cooking time: 3 minutes

Makes 15 sandwiches

unsalted butter, for greasing

approximately 1½ quarts water (check polenta package instructions for exact quantities)

9-oz box instant polenta

4 pork sausages

2 tablespoons extra virgin olive oil

5½oz Fontina, provolone, or Bel Paese cheese, thinly sliced

small handful of thyme leaves

sea salt flakes

Preheat the oven to 375°F. Grease a 15¼ x 10½-inch roasting pan with butter and line a baking pan with parchment paper.

To make the polenta, bring the water to a boil together with a handful of salt. Gradually add the polenta, stirring with a wooden spoon, and cook, stirring continuously, for 5 minutes. Remove from the heat and stir for a further 4 to 5 minutes, until the polenta has thickened but still remains easy to pour.

Pour the polenta into the prepared roasting pan and flatten it with a spatula into a ¾-inch thick layer. Let stand to cool and set for 30 minutes.

While the polenta is cooling, arrange the sausages in a baking dish, drizzle them with the oil, and bake for 30 minutes. Let the sausages cool for 10 minutes, then cut each into 10 to 12 slices to obtain 45 slices in total (3 per sandwich).

Cut the cooled polenta into 30 rectangles measuring 1 x 2 inches, or use the rim of a sherry glass to form the same number of polenta circles.

Arrange half the polenta pieces on the prepared baking pan. Top each of the arranged polenta pieces with the sausage and cheese slices and sandwich together with a second polenta piece. Bake for 10 minutes, until crisp and golden. Transfer to a serving dish, scatter with the thyme, and serve.

These mouthwatering morsels will keep in the refrigerator for up to 3 days: simply reheat them in the oven for a few minutes at 300°F.

Tramezzini

TEA SANDWICHES

The idea of stuffing bread—or making sandwiches—dates back to imperial Rome. Over the last 20 years, however, the *tramezzino* has become an expression of gastronomic creativity, with infinite fillings. Paired with a glass of local aperitif, these soft sandwiches have become a part of the Italian lifestyle. This particular example is reminiscent of the Italian flag.

Preparation time: 25 minutes plus resting

Serves 8

4 slices white sandwich bread, crusts removed

4 slices wholewheat bread, crusts removed

White cream filling:

handful of rosemary leaves, finely chopped

handful of thyme leaves, finely chopped

handful of basil leaves, finely chopped

1 cup cream cheese

Green cream filling:

$5^{1}/_{2}$oz arugula

$^{1}/_{4}$ to $^{1}/_{3}$ cup extra virgin olive oil

$^{1}/_{2}$ cup pine nuts

1 cup grated Parmesan cheese

1 cup grated pecorino romano cheese

2 garlic cloves, peeled and left whole

pinch of salt

Red cream filling:

$3^{1}/_{2}$oz smoked salmon

handful of dill fronds

$5^{1}/_{2}$oz ricotta cheese

2 tablespoons tomato paste

Line a 2-pound loaf pan (measuring $9^{1}/_{2}$ x $5^{1}/_{2}$ x $2^{1}/_{2}$ inches) with plastic wrap.

To prepare the white cream filling, stir the chopped herbs through the cream cheese in a bowl. Set aside.

To prepare the green cream filling, put the arugula and a little of the olive oil in a food processor with the rest of the ingredients. Blend together, gradually adding the remaining oil until you reach a creamy consistency. Set aside.

To prepare the red cream filling, blend the salmon, dill, ricotta, and tomato paste together in the food processor to form a smooth, creamy paste.

To assemble the sandwich loaf, arrange 2 wholewheat bread slices, trimming as necessary, to form a layer on the bottom of the loaf pan. Spread over the red cream filling evenly using a spatula, then cover with 2 white bread slices. Spread the white cream filling over evenly in the same way, then cover again with wholewheat bread slices and spread over the green cream filling. Finish with the final 2 slices of white bread.

Wrap the pan with plastic wrap and transfer to the refrigerator for 2 hours for everything to rest (if you're in a hurry you can do this in the freezer—it'll only take 30 minutes—just don't forget about it!).

Once the sandwich loaf has rested, remove the plastic wrap, invert the pan, and cut the loaf into $^{3}/_{4}$-inch slices. Enjoy with a glass of sparkling prosecco.

Alici o sardine marinate

MARINATED ANCHOVIES OR SARDINES

Go to your fish dealer to buy a silvery gray multitude of fresh anchovies or sardines—they are good for you. Ask for the heads and backbones to be removed, because there is no denying that having to prepare these little fish yourself is a pain. Your fish dealer will do it for you, with pleasure, as long as the store isn't busy—on a Saturday morning, forget it!

Preparation time: 10 minutes plus soaking

Cooking time: 30 minutes

Serves 8

1lb 2oz fresh anchovies or sardines, heads and backbones removed (ask your fish dealer to do this for you)

1¼ cups white wine vinegar

⅓ cup extra virgin olive oil, plus extra for greasing

1½ cups bread crumbs (*see* page 262)

1½ cups grated pecorino romano cheese

2 garlic cloves, grated

large handful of flat-leaf parsley leaves, very finely chopped

1oz dried oregano

salt and pepper

Place the anchovies in a bowl, cover with the vinegar, and let soak for 15 minutes.

Preheat the oven to 350°F. Grease a baking dish with a little olive oil.

Sprinkle the bread crumbs over the bottom of the baking dish in an even layer, then arrange a layer of anchovies on top and season with salt and pepper. Continue to layer the anchovies alternately with layers of the cheese, grated garlic, chopped parsley, and oregano, seasoning as you go and finishing with a layer of anchovy fillets. Pour the olive oil evenly over the anchovies and bake in the oven for 30 minutes until golden.

Enjoy the anchovies warm or cold as an *aperitivo* or use as an alternative topping for bruschetta (*see* page 46).

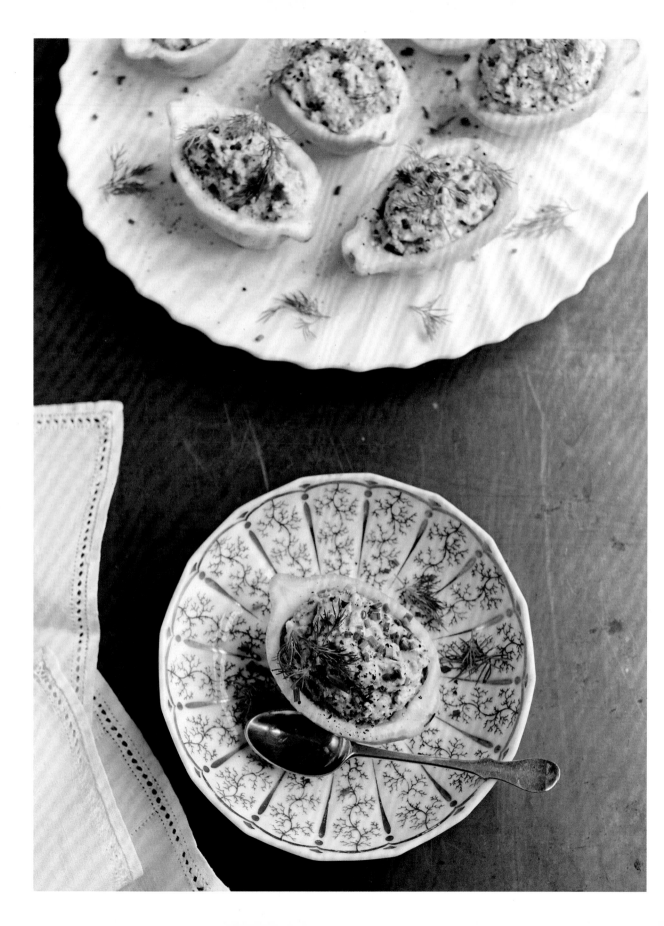

Limoni ripieni alla crema di tonno

LEMONS FILLED WITH TUNA CREAM

In a favorable climate, lemon trees flower and bear fruit four times a year. Therefore this festive citrus dish can be found on our tables all year round. The creamy filling reminds me of the more famous Pesce Finto di Natale (*see* page 222), but with the addition of mascarpone cheese. Italians like variations, after all, hardly ever sticking to a fixed plan. This luminous dish resonates with rural tradition, a nod to the little details that make life a marvelous journey. *Bella la vita, huh?*

Preparation time: 20 minutes plus chilling

Serves 4

4 large unwaxed lemons

6oz canned tuna in olive oil, drained

2 teaspoons salted capers, rinsed

$1/3$ cup mayonnaise

$1/4$ cup mascarpone cheese

$1/3$ cup pitted black olives

3 hard-boiled eggs, peeled

small handful of chives

small handful of dill fronds

$1/2$ teaspoon dried oregano

pinch of salt

pinch of white pepper

pinch of red chili flakes

To garnish

1 tablespoon snipped chives

1 tablespoon chopped dill fronds

$1/2$ teaspoon dried oregano

Halve the lemons lengthwise.

Squeeze $1/4$ cup of juice out of one lemon and set this aside, then scoop the pulp out of all the lemon halves using a teaspoon. Remove and discard the seeds and put the lemon pulp and reserved juice in a food processor together with the rest of the ingredients. Blend together well to form a thick, creamy paste.

Use a spoon or a pastry bag to fill the empty lemon halves, then scatter with the chopped herbs, and dried oregano to finish. The filled lemons can be stored in the refrigerator for up to 3 days until needed.

Chapter 6 ROMANTIC DINNERS

Anyone keen to seek out authentic Roman types should make a note of the term "*coatto.*" A *coatto* is the guy you see passing the time in the local bar or square. Restless by nature, irritated by what he perceives to be the inescapable monotony of life, he harbors strong reactions to even the most inconsequential events. He has a passion for sports in general (and for motorbikes and souped-up cars in particular), wears flashy clothes, and talks with his hands, his exaggerated gestures accompanied by laughter louder than his car stereo. He performs hilarious acts of bravado, showing off like an urban peacock for the benefit of his girlfriend and the amusement of his pals. Don't mistake his behavior for rudeness or malice; in most cases it's just the result of a misplaced lust for life and hides a good heart and a fierce sense of loyalty.

Like the majority of their countrymen, Romans don't move out of their parents' homes until they are well into their thirties. I guess *mamma*'s gnocchi are just too good to leave behind. In Italy, leaving home usually involves not only a car filled with boxes but also a precious notebook of old recipes from *nonna*, to bring out on those special occasions, like a romantic dinner. Don't panic, tradition is your savior here—after all, the best way to someone's heart is through their stomach. Every mouthful has to be delicious. Whatever you decide to cook, *don't* make it the way their mother would. You could never compete. Instead, whip out those tricks you learned from your grandma and pull it off the Roman way, by giving tradition a glossy, modern finish. Surprise them with the crispiness of Orata in Crosta di Patate (*see* page 161), assail their senses with crunchy lamb *costolette*, cauliflower, and chestnuts (*see* page 164), or embrace them with the warmth of pasta and chickpeas (*see* page 158).

Working your magic through food is a proven path to success, for both you and your guest—think of the lavish banquets of Ancient Rome, where people used to lie on their sides, lazily picking at food in a position that had the advantage of letting them doze off between courses, while the harmonious singing of the muses created a dinner scenario somewhere between reality and imagination. That's where we are headed in this chapter: romantic food to let the magic happen. Tempting and easy. Impossibly delicious.

Bucatini alle vongole e patate alla menta

BUCATINI WITH CLAMS & MINTY POTATOES

The real value of an ingredient lies in its quality—particularly true with a dish like this one. To make this saucy paradise, I visit my fish dealer and, with exquisite stubbornness, ask for the freshest clams. Once I'm home, the first thing I do is check them for sand. Arm yourself with the same devoted patience you show your significant other and tap each clam, with the opening facing down, against a cutting board. If dark sand comes out, throw the clam away. Also, get rid of those with broken shells—you only want the best. After all, it's romance you're after. This dish is best served piping hot.

Preparation time: 20 minutes plus soaking

Cooking time: 30 minutes

Serves 2

1 round red or round white potato, peeled

1lb 2oz fresh clams

2 tablespoons extra virgin olive oil, divided

2 garlic cloves, peeled and left whole

walnut-sized lump of unsalted butter

small handful of mint leaves, very finely chopped

5$\frac{1}{2}$oz bucatini or spaghetti

handful of flat-leaf parsley leaves, finely chopped

1 teaspoon salted capers, rinsed, to garnish

salt and pepper

To remove excess starch from the potato, peel it and let it soak in a bowl of water for 15 minutes, then drain it and cut it into $\frac{1}{4}$-inch cubes.

Meanwhile, put the clams in a colander and rinse them well under running water. Drain well and set aside.

Gently heat 1 tablespoon of olive oil in a large saucepan. Add one whole garlic clove and leave for 2 to 3 minutes to brown, then tip in the clams, cover with the lid, and cook over high heat for 5 minutes, or until the clams are completely open. Remove from the heat and drain the clams in a colander set over a bowl, reserving the precious cooking liquid. Extract the clam meat from half of the shells and discard any clams that haven't opened.

Add the potato cubes to a small saucepan of salted water, bring to a simmer, and cook over medium-high heat for 10 minutes until tender, then drain. Melt the butter in the same pan, add the potato pieces along with the mint, season to taste, and cook for 5 minutes more until the potatoes have softened further and the flavors have mingled together.

Bring a large saucepan of salted water to a boil, add the pasta, and cook following the package directions until *al dente*, then drain, reserving a few ladlefuls of the pasta cooking water.

While the pasta is cooking, heat the remaining olive oil in another large saucepan with the remaining whole garlic clove for 2 to 3 minutes until the garlic clove has browned, then pour in the clam cooking liquid, bring to a simmer, and cook for approximately 5 minutes or until reduced by half.

Add the drained pasta to the pan along with the shelled clams, minty potatoes, and parsley, then gradually add the reserved pasta cooking water along with the remaining clams still in their shells. Spoon into bowls and scatter with the capers to garnish.

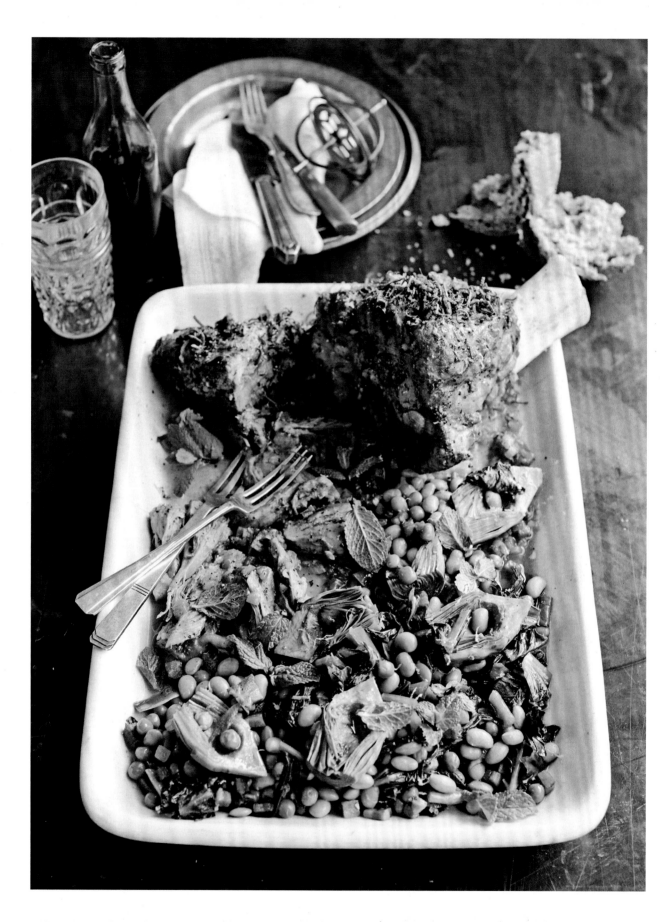

Ossobuco al pepe verde e vignarola

ROMAN-STYLE OSSOBUCO WITH VIGNAROLA

Preparation time: 15 minutes

Cooking time: 2 hours 20 minutes

Serves 2

½ cup all-purpose flour

2 organic veal shanks, about
    1½ inches thick

2 tablespoons dried green
    peppercorns

1 small carrot, peeled

1 shallot, peeled

1 celery stalk, trimmed

2 anchovies in olive oil

zest of 1 lemon

10 sage leaves

3 tablespoons extra virgin olive oil

½ stick unsalted butter

½ cup dry white wine

1 cup vegetable stock

Vignarola:

3 tablespoons extra virgin olive oil

2 teaspoons unsalted butter

2 scallions, chopped

3½oz pancetta or smoked
    bacon cubes

1⅓ cups fava beans or
    edamame, defrosted if frozen

⅔ cup garden peas, defrosted
    if frozen

3 large artichokes, cleaned
    (*see* page 13), cut into ½-inch
    slices, and placed in
    acidulated water

5½oz romaine lettuce, chopped

handful of mint leaves, divided

½ cup vegetable stock

½ cup grated pecorino
    romano cheese

salt

In a tiny side street off the imposing Via della Scrofa, there's a restaurant called La Campana. It's one of the oldest in Rome, dating back to 1518, when it offered board and travel booking services to pilgrims and foreigners. Their *vignarola* is a gift from heaven—hands down the best I've ever tasted. This stew of spring vegetables is a reminder of the unbelievable awesomeness of every little thing. There are few better things in life than dunking bread into a plate of ossobuco. This dish is a perennial favorite with lovers of Roman cuisine.

Place the flour in a plastic food bag, add the veal shanks, seal the bag securely, and shake to coat the shanks in the flour. Set the shanks aside on a plate.

Lightly crush the peppercorns in a mortar and pestle or with the flat side of a heavy knife and press them into the veal shanks.

Put the carrot, shallot, and celery in a food processor and blend together briefly until finely chopped. Set the mixture aside and repeat with the anchovies, lemon zest, and sage.

Heat the oil and butter in a Dutch oven over medium heat until the butter has melted. Add the veal shanks and brown for 2 to 3 minutes on each side, then pour in the wine, bring to a vigorous simmer, and cook for 15 minutes, until the liquid has evaporated. Add the vegetable stock, lower the heat to a gentle simmer, and let cook, covered, for about 2 hours, until the meat is falling off of the bone.

While the ossobuco is cooking, prepare the *vignarola*. Heat the oil and butter together in a large skillet over medium heat, add the scallions and pancetta, and cook, stirring, for 3 to 4 minutes until translucent. Add the fava beans, peas, artichoke slices, chopped lettuce, and half of the mint, then pour in the stock, bring to a simmer, and cook for 15 to 20 minutes, or until the liquid has reduced by half. Season with salt and sprinkle with the grated pecorino to finish.

To serve, transfer the veal pieces onto plates and pour the juices from the dish evenly over them. Spoon over the anchovy mixture, scatter with the remaining mint leaves, and serve accompanied by the *vignarola*.

Pasta e ceci, salvia e fagioli del purgatorio con tartufo nero e lardo

PASTA, CHICKPEAS & BEANS
WITH BLACK TRUFFLES & LARDO

In Rome, you might bump into a *commendatore*—a guy who acts as if he's entitled to the honors of a knight but without carrying out any of the duties. He always seems to be on to the next big deal in town, mentioning it "discreetly" to his trusted waiter, who in turn will barely mention it to the barber, a very reliable man who's married to the grocer. "Shhh! No one knows about it, *capo*!" he'll mutter, flashing his gold teeth. Then he'll turn to his bowl of *pasta e ceci*. This is an everyday dish turned into a special treat by adding black summer truffles and *lardo di Colonnata*, a cured piece of hard fat. You can find good *lardo* in Italian delis and online.

Preparation time: 10 minutes

Cooking time: 45 minutes

Serves 2

1½oz *lardo di Colonnata* or other good-quality *lardo*, thinly sliced

¼ cup extra virgin olive oil

1 garlic clove, peeled and lightly crushed with a heavy knife

1 small carrot, very finely chopped

1 shallot, very finely chopped

1 celery stalk, trimmed and very finely chopped

1 teaspoon dried rosemary

1oz pancetta or smoked bacon cubes

3 tablespoons white wine

½ cup canned cannellini beans, drained

½ cup canned chickpeas, drained

⅔ cup passata

½ cup vegetable stock

1 bay leaf

¾oz black summer truffles, cleaned and cut into thin slices, divided

5½oz chifferi rigati, ditalini, or any other short pasta

salt and pepper

Heat the *lardo* in a small nonstick skillet over medium heat for 5 minutes until crisp and crunchy. Set aside.

Gently heat the oil and crushed garlic clove together in a medium saucepan for 2 to 3 minutes, then remove the garlic clove and add the chopped carrot, shallot, celery, and rosemary. Cook for 5 minutes, stirring occasionally, then add the pancetta and cook for a further 5 minutes until the vegetables have started to soften. Add the wine, beans, and chickpeas, increase the heat, and simmer vigorously for 10 minutes until the liquid has evaporated.

Add the passata, stock, and bay leaf to the pan, bring to a gentle simmer, and cook for a further 20 minutes or until reduced by half. Transfer half the mixture to a food processor and blend to a smooth consistency similar to a purée. Return to the pan, stir in half of the truffle slices, and season with salt and pepper. Keep warm.

Bring a large saucepan of salted water to a boil, add the pasta, and cook following the package directions until *al dente*.

Drain the pasta and mix it together with the sauce. Ladle into two shallow bowls, scatter with the crunchy *lardo* pieces and remaining truffle slices, and serve piping hot.

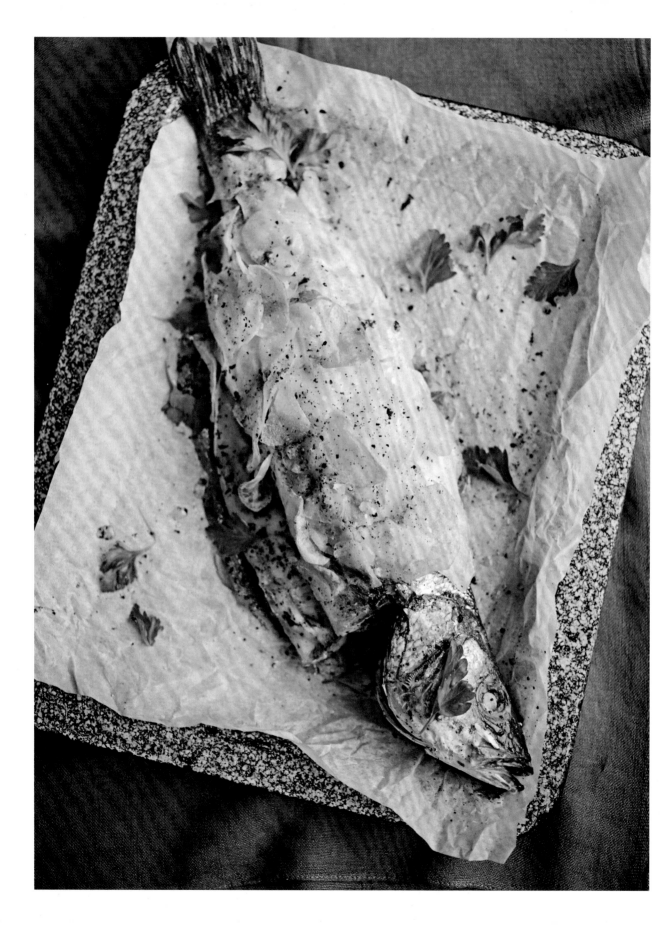

Orata in crosta di patate

SEABREAM IN A POTATO CRUST

One of my favorite spots in Rome is the courtyard of the Palazzo Spada, with its fragrant orange trees. On one side, you see a long colonnade, at the far end of which stands a life-size statue of a Roman warrior. But it's a deception, a misleadingly lifelike use of forced perspective created by the Baroque architect Borromini.

In the *trompe l'œil* style, a layer of crisp potatoes represents the scales of the fish in this dish. Here, nothing is as it seems. Have another look, and prepare your taste buds for an adventure.

Preparation time: 10 minutes plus marinating and soaking

Cooking time: 35 minutes

Serves 2

$1/2$ cup dry white wine

sprig of thyme, finely chopped

1 bay leaf, finely chopped

$1/2$ teaspoon chopped rosemary leaves

3 tablespoons chopped curly parsley leaves

3 tablespoons extra virgin olive oil, plus extra for greasing and drizzling

1 x 1lb 5-oz sea bream or sea bass, cleaned, gutted, and scaled (ask your fish dealer to do this for you)

$2^1/4$lb medium russet potatoes

$1/3$ stick unsalted butter, melted

salt and pepper

In a small bowl, stir together the wine, chopped herbs, and olive oil and season with salt and pepper. Place the sea bream in a large dish and brush inside and out with the herby marinade to ensure it is evenly coated. Transfer to the refrigerator and let marinate for 30 minutes.

Meanwhile, peel, wash, and dry the potatoes before cutting them into $1/4$-inch slices. Drop the potato slices into a bowl filled with water and let stand for 10 minutes to release any excess starch.

Drain the potatoes, then drop them into a saucepan of salted boiling water and blanch for 8 to 10 minutes. Drain again and let cool on parchment paper.

Preheat the oven to 350°F. Line a baking pan with parchment paper and grease with a little olive oil.

Arrange half the potatoes on the prepared baking pan to form a silhouette as long and as wide as the sea bream itself, season them with salt and pepper, and drizzle with a little extra oil.

Remove the fish from the marinade and place it on top of the potato layer, then arrange the remaining potatoes over the fish in an overlapping pattern as if they were scales. Brush everything with olive oil and season with salt and pepper.

Cover the head and tail of the fish with aluminum foil, spoon three-quarters of the marinade over the rest of the fish, and bake for 10 minutes. Then lower the heat to 325°F and bake for a further 10 minutes, until the fish is almost cooked through. Turn the broiler onto high, brush the fish with melted butter, and cook for a final 5 minutes until golden.

Remove the fish from the oven and transfer to a serving plate. Serve warm, with the remaining marinade in a small bowl on the side as a sauce.

Costolette d'agnello in crosta con cavolfiore e castagne accompagnate
da gattò di patate, cardi e arance

CRISPY LAMB CUTLETS WITH CAULIFLOWER & CHESTNUTS ACCOMPANIED BY A POTATO & ORANGE SAVORY CAKE

Goethe once said "see Naples and die." I like to think something like "see Rome and live better, in a fuller, more aware way, with history and personal memories running side by side, making this city your own." The city's food also speaks directly to the heart with a sense of simplicity, of living in the present moment, which is reflected in this flavorsome dish. If you can't find cardoons to make the savory cake, you can use celery, chard stems, or artichoke instead.

Preparation time: 20 minutes plus resting

Cooking time: 1 hour

Serves 2

3/4 cup all-purpose flour, plus extra for dusting

1/2 cup ground almonds

2/3 stick cold unsalted butter, cut into 1/2-inch cubes

1 teaspoon salt

1 teaspoon cold water

5 1/2oz cauliflower, trimmed and cut into 1/2-inch chunks

3 tablespoons extra virgin olive oil

1 garlic clove, peeled and left whole

1oz whole cooked chestnuts, cut into 1/2-inch chunks

4 lamb loin cutlets, frenched

1 egg yolk mixed together with 1 tablespoon milk, to glaze

1/2 cup slivered almonds

Potato and orange savory cake:

3 1/2oz cardoons, trimmed and cut into 4-inch pieces

10 1/2oz potatoes, cut into 3/4-inch chunks, plus 2 extra, thinly sliced, to decorate

In a food processor, blend together the flour, ground almonds, butter, salt, and cold water for a few seconds until combined. Transfer to a flat surface and quickly bring the ingredients together with your fingertips to form a flaky dough. You don't want to overwork it, or you'll end up with soggy pastry. Seal in plastic wrap and let rest in the refrigerator for 30 minutes.

Meanwhile, bring a large saucepan of salted water to a boil, add the cauliflower pieces, and blanch for 8 minutes until tender. Drain well and dry on a clean dish cloth.

Heat the oil in a skillet over medium heat, add the garlic, and cook, stirring, for 5 minutes until golden. Remove the garlic from the pan, add the cauliflower and chestnuts, and cook for 5 minutes, until crisp and lightly golden, then remove them from the pan and set aside. Lower the lamb cutlets into the pan and brown for 1 minute on each side. Set aside to cool, then pat dry with paper towels.

For the potato and orange savory cake, bring a saucepan of salted water to a boil, add the cardoon and potato chunks, and cook for 15 minutes. Then add the potato slices and cook for a further 5 minutes. Drain well and dry on paper towels, setting the sliced potatoes aside.

Pass the potato chunks through a potato ricer into a bowl, then add the egg, parsley, nutmeg, milk, orange juice, cardoons, and half of the butter and Parmesan. Season with salt and mix together until smooth.

Brush the surface of a 6-inch baking dish or two small individual ramekins with the oil and scatter the bottom with half the bread crumbs. Spoon over half the mashed-potato mixture, place the ham and cheese strips on top, and finish with the remaining mashed potatoes. Spread the potato slices over the surface, scatter with the rest of the Parmesan cheese and bread crumbs, and dot with the remaining butter. Set aside.

1 large egg

handful of flat-leaf parsley leaves, very finely chopped, plus extra to garnish

1 teaspoon ground nutmeg

3 tablespoons milk

zest and juice of 1 orange

1/3 stick unsalted butter, divided

1/3 cup grated Parmesan cheese, divided

2 tablespoons extra virgin olive oil

1/2 cup bread crumbs (*see* page 262), divided

1oz roast ham, thinly sliced and cut into 1/2-inch strips

1³/4oz provolone cheese, thinly sliced and cut into 1/2-inch strips

salt

Preheat the oven to 400°F.

Roll the chilled pastry out on a clean floured work surface to a thickness of 1/4 inch and cut it into four rectangles, each large enough to cover the cutlets, about 2 x 4 inches in size. Place a meat cutlet in the middle of a pastry piece, cover with a tablespoon of the cauliflower and chestnut mixture, and wrap the edges over to seal tightly in place like a parcel, leaving the rib bone outside the pastry. Repeat with the remaining cutlets, then brush each pastry "parcel" with the egg and milk glaze and scatter with the flaked almonds. Wrap the cutlet bones in aluminum foil to finish, to prevent them from burning in the oven.

Put the potato cake into the oven and cook for 5 minutes, then add the lamb cutlets and cook for 20 to 25 minutes, until the pastry on the cutlets is golden.

Remove the cutlets from the oven and set aside, then turn the broiler to high and cook the potato cake for 10 minutes more until crispy and golden. Remove the potato cake from the oven, sprinkle it with the orange zest and remaining parsley, and serve alongside the lamb cutlets.

Ravioli alla Romana con broccoli, alici, pomodori secchi e ricotta

ROMAN-STYLE RAVIOLI WITH BROCCOLI, ANCHOVIES, SUN-DRIED TOMATOES & RICOTTA

A ray of sunlight hits my favorite spot in the Biblioteca Angelica as I get lost in a book. Looking at the endless bookshelves, browsing through the card index, respecting the rule of silence—everything about this place is life-enhancing. As I leave the library, thinking that my day couldn't get any better, I see a *pastificio*. Making pasta by hand always makes me feel good. I like to experiment, so here basil-flavored pasta meets a filling of ricotta, sun-dried tomatoes, and anchovies. Free your imagination, lose yourself in eternity.

Preparation time: 30 minutes

Cooking time: 25 minutes

Serves 2

$3/4$ cup all-purpose flour

1 egg, beaten

10 basil leaves, chopped, plus extra
  to serve

pinch of salt

$3/4$ cup grated Parmesan or $2^1/2$oz
  ricotta salata cheese, grated

Filling:

4 anchovies in olive oil, drained

$4^1/2$oz ricotta cheese

10 sun-dried tomatoes

Sauce:

2 tablespoons extra virgin olive oil

2 anchovies in olive oil, drained

7oz purple broccoli, coarsely
  chopped

pinch of red chile flakes

$2/3$ cup vegetable stock

$1/2$ cup walnut pieces, divided

For the filling, put all the ingredients in a food processor and blend together until well combined. Cover and refrigerate until needed.

For the sauce, gently heat the olive oil and the anchovies together in a skillet over medium heat for 5 minutes, stirring occasionally, until the anchovies have dissolved. Add the broccoli pieces to the pan together with the red chile flakes, stock, and half the walnut pieces, bring to a simmer, and cook for 15 minutes, until the broccoli pieces are tender and the liquid has reduced by one-third.

Meanwhile, make the egg pasta dough. Place the flour on a large board or a clean, floured work surface. Make a well in the center and put the beaten egg, chopped basil leaves, and salt in it.

Using the tips of your fingers, mix the eggs with the flour, incorporating a little at a time, until everything is combined. Knead the pieces of dough together until you have one big, smooth lump of dough, then divide it into two pieces.

Using a rolling pin, roll one dough portion out to a thickness of $1/16$-inch and into a rectangle 14 x 9 inches in size. Working quickly, place teaspoonfuls of filling 1 inch apart over one half of the pasta sheet and brush lightly around the filling with water to moisten. Fold the sheet over and press down around the fillings to seal, then cut out the ravioli squares around the filling using a pastry wheel. Repeat with the remaining dough and filling.

Bring a large saucepan of salted water to a boil, add the ravioli, and cook for 3 minutes, or until they float to the surface. As the ravioli are ready, scoop them up with a slotted spoon and transfer them to a large bowl along with half the broccoli sauce and a ladleful of the pasta cooking water. Once you have fished out all the ravioli, add the rest of the sauce, sprinkle with the grated Parmesan, remaining walnuts, and a few extra basil leaves to serve.

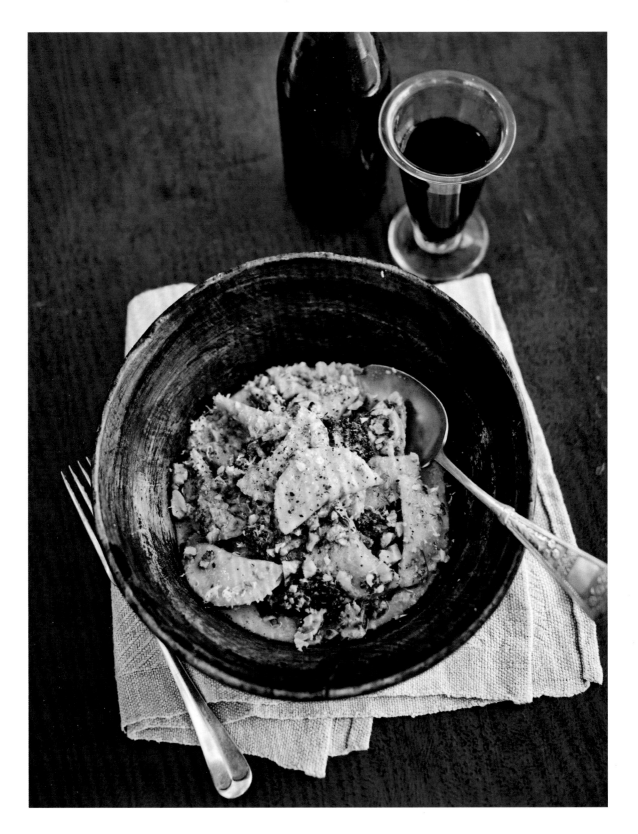

Spiedini di anguille in foglie di alloro e salsa al cren

EEL & BAY LEAF SKEWERS WITH HOMEMADE HORSERADISH SAUCE

In the days of the Roman Empire, a victorious military commander was crowned with a laurel wreath. An officer would recite the *memento mori*—bear in mind that one day you will die—to remind him that glory was only temporary. *Abbassa la cresta*, you'd better lower your crest, as we would say today to those who think too highly of themselves.
It's worth trying to find fresh horseradish root for this recipe—try ethnic supermarkets or a farmers' market—but you can always buy ready-made horseradish sauce.

Preparation time: 15 minutes plus marinating

Cooking time: 10 to 15 minutes

Serves 2

14oz fresh eels, skinned, gutted, boned, and cut into 2-inch logs (ask your fish dealer to do this for you)

1/3 cup extra virgin olive oil

1 garlic clove, peeled and left whole

1 1/2 cups dry white wine

10 black peppercorns

12 bay leaves

large handful of finely chopped curly parsley leaves

Sauce:

1/4 cup freshly grated horseradish root

1 tablespoon white wine vinegar

1 teaspoon superfine sugar

1 tablespoon extra virgin olive oil

1 tablespoon bread crumbs (*see* page 262)

Combine the eel pieces in a large plastic food bag with the oil, garlic, wine, and peppercorns. Seal the bag securely, shake well, and let marinate in the refrigerator for 2 hours.

While the eel is marinating, soak six bamboo skewers in water (this will prevent them from burning during cooking).

Preheat the broiler to high.

Remove the eel pieces from the marinade, reserving the liquid. Alternately thread two pieces of fish and two bay leaves onto each skewer and brush each with the marinade. Lay the skewers on the middle rack of the oven and broil for 10 to 15 minutes, turning and brushing the eel with the marinade halfway through cooking, until the eel pieces are charred and cooked through.

Meanwhile, prepare the sauce by mixing the grated horseradish, vinegar, sugar, oil, and bread crumbs together in a bowl until well combined.

Arrange the skewers on plates, scatter with the chopped parsley, and serve alongside the creamed horseradish sauce and a Puntarelle Salad (*see* page 120), if you like.

Penne gratinate alla Campolattaro

CAMPOLATTARO-STYLE PENNE GRATIN

Mirror, mirror on the wall, who is the fairest of them all? I love how simple ingredients can turn into something spectacular. It's the 29th of June. Outside, choirs and street bands celebrate the Feast of St. Peter and St. Paul, observed in Rome as a public holiday. Indoors, there is the aroma of enchanting creaminess. Simmer, poach, fry. Soften, sift, emulsify. Comforting gestures to help get the most out of everyday life. Keeping it light while making a desirable pasta dish. Staying in is the new going out.

Preparation time: 10 minutes

Cooking time: 45 minutes

Serves 2

2 tablespoons extra virgin olive oil

1 x 3^1/$_2$-oz chicken breast, cut into
^{1}/$_2$-inch slices

^{1}/$_2$oz black truffle, finely sliced

1^3/$_4$oz prosciutto, finely sliced

2 tablespoons Cognac

^{1}/$_3$ cup heavy cream

1 cup grated Parmesan cheese,
divided

5^1/$_2$oz penne rigate pasta

^{1}/$_2$ cup bread crumbs (*see*
page 262)

^{1}/$_4$ stick unsalted butter, cut
into ^{1}/$_4$-inch cubes

salt and pepper

Heat the oil in a small nonstick skillet over medium heat, add the chicken pieces, and cook, stirring, for 5 to 7 minutes, until the chicken is lightly browned and cooked through. Add the truffle, prosciutto, and Cognac to the pan, bring to a simmer, and cook for 5 minutes until the liquid has evaporated. Stir in the cream and half the Parmesan and remove the pan from the heat.

Tip half of the sauce into a food processor and blend until smooth. Return to the pan and stir everything together well.

Preheat the oven to 350°F.

Bring a saucepan of salted water to a boil, add the penne, and cook for half the time suggested on the package, then drain the pasta and pour it into a small baking dish. Add the sauce, season with salt and pepper, and mix well. Scatter with the bread crumbs and remaining Parmesan and dot with the butter.

Bake the penne gratin for 30 minutes until the crust is golden and crisp. Let rest for 10 minutes before serving with a green salad.

Seppioline piselli, avocado e pomodoro

SQUID WITH PEAS, AVOCADO & TOMATOES

This piquantly spicy dish facilitates the best conversations, the kind you normally wouldn't even dream of having without it as a go-between. That's the miracle of partaking of a meal together: there's a solemn sense of ceremony and people are at once very eager to listen and thrilled to speak, their intentions heightened by sharing an intimate moment. Life may be a pantomime, but dinner . . . that's serious stuff.

Preparation time: 15 minutes plus marinating

Cooking time: 1 hour 25 minutes

Serves 4 for a double date

2¼ lb squid or baby squid, cleaned and tentacles separated (ask your fish dealer to do this for you)

3 tablespoons extra virgin olive oil, divided

juice of 1 lemon

small handful of curly parsley leaves, very finely chopped, plus extra to garnish

small handful of cilantro leaves, very finely chopped, plus extra to garnish

1 red onion, finely chopped

1 garlic clove

1 celery stalk, trimmed and finely chopped

½ cup dry white wine

2 cups cherry tomatoes, halved

2⅓ cups garden peas, defrosted if frozen

2 cups vegetable stock

1 avocado, seeded and cut ½-inch cubes

½ teaspoon Tabasco sauce

salt

Take a squid tube and place a large chef's knife flat inside it. Using a second knife, slice the squid three times on each side, as if you're cutting it into rings (you won't be able to cut all the way because of the other knife).

Place the prepared squid tubes along with the tentacles in a resealable food bag with half the olive oil, the lemon juice, parsley, and cilantro. Seal the bag and place in the refrigerator to marinate for 2 hours.

When ready to cook, heat the rest of the oil in a large nonstick skillet over low heat, and add the onion, garlic, and celery. Cook, stirring, for 10 minutes, until soft and translucent. Remove the squid from the marinade and add it to the pan together with the wine and tomatoes. Increase the heat to high, bring to a vigorous simmer, and cook, stirring, for 15 minutes, until all the liquid has evaporated.

Reduce the heat to low, season with salt, and add the peas and stock to the pan. Simmer very gently, stirring occasionally, for 45 minutes, then stir in the avocado pieces and the remaining lemon juice and cook for a further 15 minutes, until the sauce is thick and the squid is tender.

Remove the squid from the heat and let cool slightly before stirring in the Tabasco sauce. Scatter with the rest of the fresh herbs and serve with a dry white wine, such as Soave or Pinot Grigio.

Any leftovers can be kept in the refrigerator for up to 3 days.

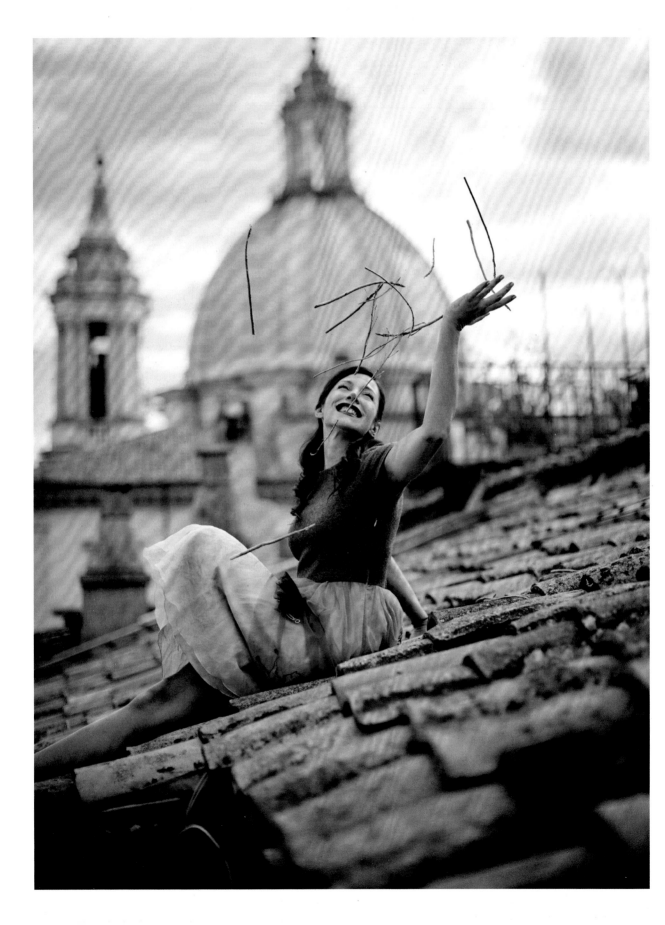

Chapter 7 #FOODHAPPINESS SUPPERS

Italy is sometimes known as the land of Cockaigne, an ideal place where prosperity, abundance, and gratification are available to everyone. It's easy to believe—just keep your eyes closed and dream on.

There is a powerful magic among people sharing a meal. Personal anecdotes mix and whirl audaciously while diners relish their pasta. Perhaps it's because they find themselves repeating a ritual linked to the history of the dish itself. I myself always feel the need to understand the origins of what I'm biting into, and that's why, at my table, I strive for authenticity and time-honored tradition. There's an honesty about eating together, and it is without a doubt one of the most straightforward ways of appreciating our relationships with those we love. Everyone is more like themselves at the dining table. We eat together when we want to spend quality time in someone's company.

Sharing food is not simply about that almost inevitable stain on the tablecloth after enjoying a good Pollo alla Romana (*see* page 179). Crucially, it leaves us intensely exposed to others. Often this happens without us even noticing, but I believe it doesn't go unnoticed by our soul. The more the ingredients respond to the truest nature of the dish, the more we are bound to have a heartfelt experience. And that's what #foodhappiness is all about: it's that grin on people's faces, their eager anticipation when they're presented with a dish full of promise. It's that reflective pause, the overwhelming contemplation, the thrilled expectation—#foodhappiness brings out the best in everyone.

It's also linked to art, but please don't mistake this with some chef's habit of putting big food in small dishes. No, it's another art I refer to: the winning skill of *arrangiarsi*, of making do—producing a miraculous dish using only three ingredients or transforming leftovers into something even more delicious. Back in the 1970s, a group of Italian painters including Mario Schifano and Renato Guttuso used to draw on the paper tablecloths of the Roman trattoria they used as their personal canteen. In return for these sketches, they would get a plate of pasta, a bottle of wine, and the host's eternal gratitude for having boosted the standing of his restaurant. Old recipes, new meanings. A blast from the past carrying contemporary values.

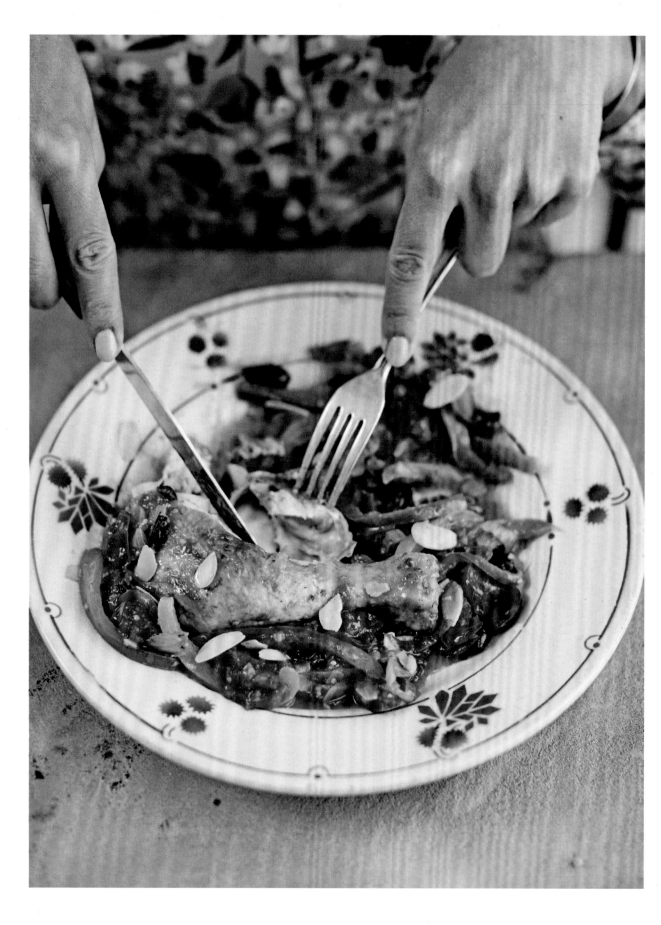

Pollo alla Romana con peperoni

ROMAN-STYLE CHICKEN WITH BELL PEPPERS

Sora Lella used to go to the Campo dei Fiori market every single day. Even if the grocer told her *"È speciale!"* she would taste each ingredient and, if satisfied, buy a whole case. Back at her restaurant, on the Isola Tiberina, she made classic Roman dishes: "I beg of you, when in Rome, the only way to have your chicken is Roman style!" What's special about this dish is the sweet and sour taste of the peppers melting into the chicken. My own twist on this dish is the addition of pungent black olives and some flaked almonds scattered on top. A spellbinding crunchy delight for an unforgettable bite.

Preparation time: 10 minutes

Cooking time: 45 minutes

Serves 6

¼ cup extra virgin olive oil, divided

1 large white onion, finely chopped, divided

1 x 4 ½-lb freerange chicken, cut into pieces, or the equivalent amount of chicken pieces

½ cup white wine

1lb 2oz baby plum or large vine tomatoes, diced, divided

1 large red bell pepper, cored, seeded, and cut into thin strips

1 large green bell pepper, cored, seeded, and cut into thin strips

1 large yellow bell pepper, cored, seeded, and cut into thin strips

⅔ cup black pitted olives

handful of basil leaves

½ cup slivered almonds

salt and pepper

Heat half the oil and onion in a saucepan over medium heat for 3 to 4 minutes, until the onion has softened and browned.

Add the chicken pieces to the pan and season with a little salt and pepper. Cook, stirring occasionally, for 10 minutes, until the chicken is lightly browned on all sides. Add the wine, bring to a vigorous simmer, and let it evaporate, then add half the tomatoes and reduce the heat to low. Let simmer gently for 30 minutes, until the chicken pieces are tender and cooked through (you can judge this by cutting into the largest pieces with a knife—if the center is no longer pink, the chicken is ready).

Meanwhile, heat the remaining oil and onion in a separate saucepan until the onion has browned. Add the bell peppers and cook for 5 minutes, stirring, until softened, then add the olives, basil, and the rest of the tomatoes. Simmer gently for 30 minutes while the chicken is cooking.

Remove both the chicken and bell-pepper mixtures from the heat and combine the two together. Let cool slightly before serving scattered with slivered almonds.

Pasta cacio, pepe e cozze

PASTA WITH CHEESE, PEPPER & MUSSELS

As much as I love seafood, the idea of cleaning mussels myself was a real turn-off, but it's really not that hard. The rope-grown mussels you find in good supermarkets are fairly clean already, so just rinse them under cold running water, then remove any remaining "beards," as those stringy threads that cling to the outside of the shell are known. If you come across a stubborn one, take hold of it with a dry piece of paper towel and pull it downward until it comes out. If you find a wide-open mussel in your batch, check if it's still alive by tapping it against another mussel, *tlack tlack tlack*. The mussel should gradually close up. If it doesn't, you've got a dead one. Discard it and move on: it's time to make that creamy sauce now.

Preparation time: 20 minutes

Cooking time: 15 minutes

Serves 4

3 tablespoons extra virgin olive oil, divided

1 garlic clove, peeled and left whole

large handful of flat-leaf parsley leaves, finely chopped, divided

handful of dill, finely chopped, divided

1lb 9oz rope-grown mussels, cleaned and beards removed (see above)

14oz farfalle or pappardelle pasta

1½ cups very finely grated pecorino romano cheese

⅔ cup roasted peanuts

salt and pepper

Heat 2 tablespoons of the olive oil in a nonstick skillet over low heat, add the garlic, and cook for 2 to 3 minutes until lightly browned.

Add half the chopped parsley and dill to the pan along with the mussels. Increase the heat to medium, cover with a lid, and cook for 5 minutes, or until the mussels have opened fully.

Tip the mussels into a colander set above a bowl. Discard any that haven't opened and reserve the mussel cooking liquid that gathers in the bowl. You can extract the mussel meat and discard the shells, if you prefer, or leave the mussels in their shells.

Bring a large saucepan of lightly salted water to a boil, add the pasta, and cook following the package directions until a few minutes before *al dente*.

While the pasta is cooking, mix together the grated pecorino with a ladleful or so of the pasta cooking water and whizz everything together with a hand-held blender to form a creamy sauce. Season with pepper and set aside. Heat the remaining tablespoon of olive oil in a saucepan over medium heat, add the mussel cooking liquid, and simmer for 1 minute until slightly thickened and reduced.

Drain the cooked pasta, reserving four ladlefuls of the pasta cooking water, and transfer it to the saucepan with the mussel cooking liquid. Add the cooked mussels, pecorino sauce, and peanuts, and scatter with the remaining herbs. Gradually add the pasta water, stirring, until the sauce is thick and creamy. Season generously with pepper and serve.

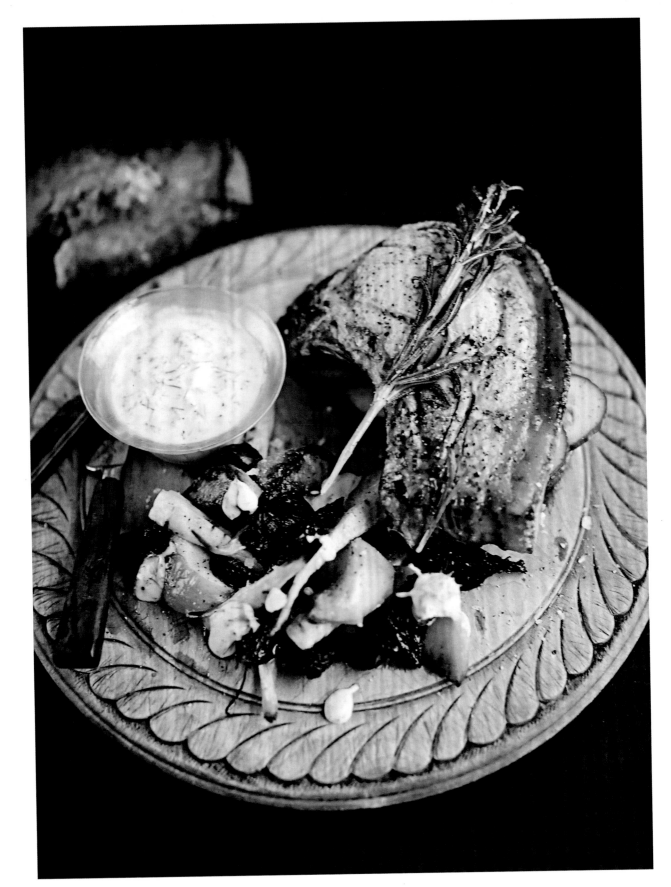

Braciole di maiale con panuntelle
PORK CHOPS WITH GREASED BREAD

Preparation time: 10 minutes plus marinating

Cooking time: 40 minutes

Serves 6

6 pork chops

$1/3$ cup extra virgin olive oil

3 garlic cloves, peeled and left whole

small handful of rosemary leaves, plus extra sprigs to garnish

2 tablespoons lemon juice

$1^{1}/_{2}$ cups dry white wine

15 black peppercorns

4 juniper berries

6 slices of rustic bread

2 cucumbers, trimmed and thinly sliced

salt and pepper

Salad:

9oz parsnips, peeled and cut into wedges

9oz baby beets, peeled and cut into wedges

2 cooking apples, peeled, cored, and cut into wedges

1 tablespoon extra virgin olive oil

Dressing:

$2/3$ cup plain yogurt

1 tablespoon white wine vinegar

juice of $1/2$ lemon

small handful of dill fronds

2 tablespoons extra virgin olive oil

This is a humble yet intensely flavored pork chop recipe. *Panuntella* means greased bread: place your pork chops (with a nice ring of fat around them) on a broiler rack over slices of good rustic bread and let the drippings transform it as the pork gently cooks. Serve with a colorful wintery salad, made all the more desirable by its freshness. Embark on a wonderful food affair.

Place the pork chops in a large resealable food bag with the oil, garlic, rosemary, lemon juice, wine, peppercorns, and juniper berries. Seal securely and shake to mix everything together well, then transfer to the refrigerator and let marinate for 1 hour.

Preheat the oven to 400°F.

While the pork chops are marinating, prepare the salad. Arrange the parsnip, beet, and apple wedges in a large roasting pan, drizzle with the olive oil, and bake in the oven for 25 minutes, turning halfway during cooking, until softened. Remove from the oven, season with salt and pepper, and let cool.

Switch the oven setting to a high broil.

For the dressing, mix all the ingredients together in a small bowl. Season with salt and pepper.

Remove the pork chops from the marinade and place them on a broiler rack under the hot broiler, arranging the pieces of bread in an ovenproof dish or baking pan directly below the chops to catch all the delicious cooking juices. Cook for 15 minutes, turning the chops halfway, until golden and cooked through.

Remove the chops and bread slices from the oven. Cover the bread with the cucumber slices, then arrange the pork chops on top and finish each piece with a sprig of rosemary. Season with salt and pepper. Toss the salad in the dressing to coat and serve alongside the chops and bread.

Tesoro di riso e sogliole con salsa al prosecco

RICE & LEMON SOLE TIMBALE
WITH PROSECCO GRAVY

Here is a flamboyant dish that will capture everyone's attention—the wow factor is assured. This dish encapsulates #foodhappiness at its best. With a *timballo*, any night is a big night. Ask your fish dealer to save the bones when preparing the sole fillets, because they will make a good addition to the stock.

Preparation time: 10 minutes

Cooking time: 1¼ hours

Serves 10

olive oil, for greasing

1 stick unsalted butter, divided

1 shallot, finely sliced

3½ cups carnaroli or arborio risotto rice

2 cups grated Parmesan cheese

½ teaspoon white pepper

¾ cup all-purpose flour

1 teaspoon ground nutmeg

1¼ cups light cream

2 cups prosecco

7 x 3½-oz lemon sole fillets, boned and skinned (ask your fish dealer to do this for you)

zest of 1 orange, cut into thin matchsticks

zest of 1 lemon, cut into thin matchsticks

salt and pepper

Stock:

3 quarts water

1 carrot

1 celery stalk, trimmed

1 large white onion

handful of curly parsley leaves

salt

For the stock, pour the measured water into a large saucepan and add the carrot, celery, onion, and parsley along with any fish bones you may have reserved from the sole. Season generously with salt and simmer over medium heat for 30 minutes or so, until the stock has reduced by one-third. Keep warm over low heat.

Preheat the oven to 400°F. Grease a nonstick 10-inch fluted bundt pan with a drizzle of olive oil.

Melt a walnut-sized lump of butter in a heavy saucepan, add the shallot, and cook over medium heat for 10 minutes until soft. Add the rice and cook, stirring, for 2 to 3 minutes until translucent, then add a ladleful of the hot stock. Season generously with salt and continue to cook over medium heat, stirring, until all the stock has been absorbed. Keep adding ladlefuls of stock, stirring constantly, allowing each ladleful to be absorbed before adding the next, until the rice no longer has a pale core and is soft but still retains a slight bite. This will take approximately 15 minutes.

Remove the risotto from the heat and add the Parmesan, pepper, and a walnut-sized lump of butter. Set aside.

In a separate small saucepan, melt the remaining butter and whisk in the flour to form a paste (roux). Stirring all the while, slowly add the nutmeg, cream, prosecco, and enough fish stock to make a smooth, pale gravy. Simmer gently for 5 minutes over low heat to thicken slightly, then remove from the heat and set aside.

Press the sole fillets against the bottom and sides of the prepared bundt pan to line it, leaving the fillets overhanging slightly at the top. Season well with salt and pepper. Spoon the risotto into the mold, pressing it down with the back of a spoon to pack it as tightly as possible, then pour over half the prosecco gravy. Carefully transfer the pan to the oven and bake for 15 to 20 minutes until lightly golden and set.

Remove from the oven and let rest for 30 minutes before carefully turning out onto a large serving dish. Scatter with the zest strips and serve with the remaining gravy.

Porchetta di Ariccia e cavoli trascinati

ARICCIA-STYLE ROAST PORK WITH "DRAGGED" SAVOY CABBAGE

In Rome, people of all kinds mix in an almost contradictory way: you see the vagabond with the prince, the lawyer with the butcher, the florist with that mysterious lady always dressed in black. It might be due to the sweet air, or the typical disposition of the native Romans, who are hardly shocked by anything, ever. Just look at the way most of them walk—*trascinati*, almost as if dragged along by an invisible force, a form of vigorous sloth.

Porchetta is one of those dishes that tastes even better a couple of days after it has been made. It can be served in slices as a main course, but in Rome it is usually consumed in a sandwich bought from a street vendor. After testing this recipe numerous times—and ending up with a smelly oven and smellier hair—I finally found a way to achieve the ultimate pleasure of this dish while keeping the oven in a decent state and my mascara intact.

About the cabbage: I know this sounds like a British side dish but it is, as we Italians say, *per davvero*, no joke. I love cabbage, and the combination with the loveliest melting pork really makes my heart sing. *Porchetta* and cabbage—a love affair of guilty pleasures.

Preparation time: 30 minutes

Cooking time: 2½ hours

Serves 10

1 x 3-lb boned pork belly, rind left on

small handful of rosemary leaves, divided

large handful of sage leaves, chopped, divided

2 teaspoons dried oregano, divided

1 tablespoon fennel seeds, divided

2 teaspoons ground nutmeg, divided

1 x 4½-lb boneless pork loin

⅓ cup extra virgin olive oil

salt and pepper

Place the pork belly skin-side up on a cutting board. Holding the blade of a sharp knife parallel to the board, cut along the length of the belly but not all the way through. Unfold the belly so that it opens like a book, then rub over one-third of the herbs and spices and season generously with salt and pepper.

Place the pork loin in the middle of the belly, season with salt and pepper and rub over another third of the herbs and spices. Roll the pork belly around the loin into a cylindrical shape and tie everything firmly together with kitchen string. Using a very sharp knife, score the skin in a diagonal pattern, then wrap everything with aluminum foil before tying it firmly with kitchen string once more.

Bring a large Dutch oven of salted water to a boil. Reduce the heat to simmering, lower the *porchetta* into the water, and let cook over low–medium heat, covered, for 1 hour. Then carefully remove the *porchetta* from the water and let cool for 10 to 15 minutes.

Coat the bottom of a large baking dish with the olive oil and remaining herbs and spices. Preheat the oven to 400°F.

Once the *porchetta* is cool, remove the aluminum foil. Place it in the prepared baking dish and roast for 1 hour until the skin is crispy and golden. Remove from the oven and let cool for 30 minutes.

Cabbage:

1 whole Savoy cabbage, trimmed

10 small new potatoes

1/2 cup extra virgin olive oil

2 garlic cloves, peeled and left whole

3 white rustic bread slices, cut into 1/2-inch cubes

salt

While the *porchetta* is cooling, make the cabbage. Remove ten large external leaves from the cabbage (these will serve as shells for the dish itself) and coarsely cut the remainder into 3/4-inch chunks.

Bring a large pot of salted water to a boil. Add the potatoes and cook for 5 minutes, then add the cabbage pieces and leaves to the pan and boil for a further 5 minutes. Drain and let cool.

When the cabbage leaves are cool enough to handle, wring out any excess water with your hands and form the leaves into 10 equal-sized balls. Peel the potatoes and cut them into 1/4-inch chunks.

Heat the oil in a large skillet over medium heat. Add the garlic cloves and cook, stirring occasionally, for 5 minutes until golden. Remove the garlic from the pan, add the bread cubes, and cook for 3 minutes until lightly browned, then add the cabbage balls and the potato chunks and cook over a medium-low heat, stirring gently, for 15 minutes. Season with salt, then remove from the heat.

Arrange a few tablespoons of the cabbage and potato mixture in the center of the reserved cabbage leaves and serve alongside the *porchetta*, cut into thick slices.

Maccheroni alla Gricia con carciofi, zucchine e ricotta salata

MACCHERONI WITH ARTICHOKES, ZUCCHINI & RICOTTA SALATA

I nearly collapsed in surprise when I found out that this recipe, which is considered the forerunner of Amatriciana sauce (*see* opposite), is almost 1,000 years old. In the past, country folks would sell their cheese at the market and keep any leftover ricotta for themselves, letting it dry and adding salt to preserve it for longer. They would then add this *ricotta salata*—which can be found in most Italian delis—to their pasta. This sauce can turn into stringy mush if you're not careful, so make sure to grate the ricotta as finely as possible.

Preparation time: 25 minutes

Cooking time: 35 to 45 minutes

Serves 6

3 zucchini, finely sliced

1/2 cup vegetable oil

3 tablespoons extra virgin olive oil

1 garlic clove, peeled and left whole

handful of mint leaves, finely chopped

5 fresh artichokes, cleaned (*see* page 13) and cut into 1/2-inch slices, or 7oz canned artichoke hearts

20 black peppercorns

9oz *guanciale*, cut into 1/4-inch cubes

1lb 2oz calamarata, garganelli, or maccheroni pasta

6oz *ricotta salata dura* or 1 2/3 cups grated Parmesan cheese

salt

Cut the zucchini into matchsticks and pat dry with paper towels to absorb any excess water.

Heat the vegetable oil in a large nonstick skillet or deep-fryer to 350 to 375°F or until a cube of bread dropped into the oil browns in 30 seconds. Carefully lower the zucchini pieces into the hot oil and cook for 5 to 6 minutes until brown and crispy. Remove from the oil, drain on paper towels, and season with salt. Set aside.

Heat the olive oil in a small saucepan over medium heat, add the garlic, mint, and artichokes and cook for 5 minutes (if you're using fresh artichokes, add a ladleful of boiling water and cook for a further 5 to 10 minutes to ensure the artichoke pieces are tender).

Toast the peppercorns in a small nonstick skillet for 5 minutes over medium heat, then coarsely crush them with the side of a heavy knife.

Heat a heavy skillet or cast-iron frying pan over medium heat, add the *guanciale* pieces, and let fry in their own fat, stirring occasionally, for 10 minutes or until crispy.

Bring a large saucepan of salted water to a boil. Add the pasta and cook following the package directions until *al dente*. Drain, reserving 2/3 cup of the pasta cooking water.

Transfer the grated *ricotta salata* to a food processor and whiz for about 10 seconds—you want the cheese to be as finely grated as possible. Place the ricotta in a small bowl and mix it together with a ladleful of the reserved pasta cooking water and half the crushed peppercorns until nice and creamy.

Mix together the pasta and the artichoke mixture, then pour the creamy ricotta sauce over it. Add a ladleful of the cooking water and stir everything together until the sauce is loose and velvety in texture. To finish, mix in the *guanciale* and serve topped with the deep-fried zucchini and the remaining crushed peppercorns.

Pasta all'Amatriciana

PASTA WITH AMATRICIANA SAUCE

This masterpiece of the Roman kitchen—topped with *guanciale*, cured pork cheek—reminds me of a popular Roman song. Take any *osteria* on the outskirts of the city on a Friday night: a group of Romans of all ages, piping hot pasta all'Amatriciana, a straw-wrapped *fiasco* of wine, and a chorus of *La Società dei Magnaccioni*—the Society of Big Eaters:

La società de li magnaccioni, (This is the Big Eaters Society)
La società de la gioventù, (This is the society fit for youth)
A noi ce piace de magnà e beve, (We love to eat and drink)
E nun ce piace de lavorà. (And we don't like to work)

Preparation time: 5 minutes

Cooking time: 35 minutes

Serves 6

9oz *guanciale,* cut into
⅟₄-inch cubes

2 tablespoons extra virgin olive oil

sprig of thyme

1 small banana shallot, finely sliced

1lb 2oz peeled plum tomatoes

½ teaspoon superfine sugar

pinch of red chili flakes

1lb 2oz bucatini, rigatoni, or
mezze maniche pasta

2½ cups grated pecorino
romano cheese

salt

Heat a heavy skillet or cast-iron frying pan over medium heat, add the *guanciale* pieces, and let fry in their own fat, stirring occasionally, for 10 minutes until crispy.

Gently heat the olive oil together with the thyme in a separate large nonstick skillet. Add the shallot and cook, stirring, for 5 minutes until softened, then add the tomatoes, breaking them up with the back of a wooden spoon. Stir in the sugar and red chili flakes and simmer over medium-low heat for 15 minutes until the sauce has thickened and reduced and the flavors have come together.

Meanwhile, bring a large saucepan of salted water to a boil. Add the pasta and cook following the package directions until *al dente*, then drain, reserving a cupful of the pasta cooking water.

Add the cooked pasta to the sauce along with half the *guanciale* and its fat. Mix everything together well, adding a little of the cooking water and the remaining *guanciale* fat as you go, until the pasta sauce is loose and velvety in texture. Transfer to a serving dish, sprinkle with the pecorino and the remaining *guanciale*, and serve immediately.

Coniglio brodettato della vendemmia con uva e olive

STEWED RABBIT WITH GRAPES & OLIVES

It's September. Harvest time. Time to taste the *novello*—a light, fruity young wine ready to drink in October—or perhaps the *sincero*, which means candid and makes you tipsy before you know it. As the Ancient Romans put it, *in vino veritas*. A *novello* wine can accompany a simple meal or help me in the kitchen. Roman wine doesn't cost a fortune. I keep a bottle with the oil and vinegar, in easy reach, while I'm cooking. Its origins lie in the Roman countryside, home to the Etruscan civilization: places like Frascati, Tarquinia, or Cerveteri, home to the Sarcophagus of the Spouses, an ancient terracotta sarcophagus in the form of a couple lounging at a banquet. In my eyes, it is one of the most democratic celebrations of love. Like the blush of a summer sunset on a vineyard flecked with gold and purple.

Preparation time: 10 minutes

Cooking time: 1 hour

Serves 6

¼ cup extra virgin olive oil

1 x 3¼-lb rabbit, cut into 8 pieces

1 large white onion, chopped

1 garlic clove, crushed

2 bay leaves, plus extra to garnish

handful of sage leaves, coarsely chopped

½ cup young red wine

1¼ cups pitted black olives

approximately 1 cup vegetable stock

3½oz red grapes

2¼oz wild arugula, plus extra to garnish

salt and pepper

Heat the oil in a large heavy saucepan over low heat. Add the rabbit pieces and cook for 10 minutes, turning them over halfway through cooking, until lightly golden all over.

Add the onion, garlic, bay leaves, and sage to the pan and season with salt and pepper. Cook, stirring, for 10 minutes until the onion has softened, then pour in the wine, add the olives, and bring to a simmer. Cook uncovered over low heat for 30 to 35 minutes, stirring occasionally and adding a ladleful of stock whenever the stew looks in danger of drying out.

Stir the grapes and arugula into the stew and cook for a final 10 minutes, until the stew is thick and glossy and the rabbit meat is falling off of the bone.

To serve, scatter a handful of arugula onto an oval serving dish. Spoon the stew on top of the arugula, and scatter some extra arugula on top. Decorate one end of the serving dish with the bay leaves, giving your rabbit stew a "crown." Serve with a simple green salad and plenty of bread for mopping up the sauce.

Ribollita Laziale

LAZIO-STYLE RIBOLLITA SOUP

This soup—the perfect example of *cucina povera*—was originally made using up leftover vegetables. With the addition of crunchy water chestnuts, my *ribollita* challenges the norm. It does take a while to prepare but it's stress-free. To give your soup extra depth, ask your butcher for some beef bones or pork rind to add to the beans. Wash, chop, and chuck everything into a pot: preparing this soup has a meditative quality. It's not your average soup.

Preparation time: 20 minutes plus overnight soaking

Cooking time: 2 hours

Serves 8

1¼ cups dried navy beans

1 teaspoon baking soda

2 quarts water

1 x approximately 1lb 2-oz beef shank bone or pork rind (optional)

1 large carrot

1 large white onion

1 celery stalk, trimmed

1 leek, trimmed and cleaned

9oz kale, trimmed

9oz cauliflower, stalk removed

2 large waxy salad potatoes

7oz Swiss chard, trimmed

9oz Savoy cabbage, trimmed

9oz cavolo nero, trimmed

¼ cup extra virgin olive oil

⅔ cup canned peeled tomatoes

small handful of fresh mixed herbs (thyme, rosemary, sage, and bay leaves), tied together with string

7oz whole water chestnuts, coarsely chopped

7oz rustic bread, cut into 8 slices

salt and pepper

Place the navy beans in a large bowl, add the baking soda, and cover with water. Let soak overnight.

When ready to cook, drain the soaked beans well. Pour the measured water into a large stockpot and bring to a boil. Add the navy beans and beef bone or pork rind, if using, and cook, covered, for 1 hour. Remove the beans from the pan using a slotted spoon and reserve the cooking liquid.

Finely chop all the vegetables either by hand or, to save time, in batches in the food processor.

Heat the oil in a large Dutch oven over low heat, add the chopped carrot, onion, celery, and leek and cook, stirring, for 10 minutes until the vegetables are softened and translucent. Add the tomatoes and fresh herb bundle along with the rest of the chopped vegetables and half the bean cooking liquid. Bring to a boil, then reduce the heat to a simmer and let cook gently for 50 minutes, adding the chopped water chestnuts halfway through cooking.

Tip half the beans into a food processor and blend to a smooth purée. Add the puréed beans to the soup along with the whole beans, season to taste, and remove from the heat. Season with salt and pepper.

Remove and discard the herb bundle from the soup. Pour half the soup into the food processor and blend until smooth, then add to the remainder and mix together well.

Line each soup bowl with a piece of bread and ladle over the *ribollita* to serve.

Chapter 8 FESTIVITIES

After the Second World War, Hollywood came to Rome, moving its sets to the Cinecittà film studios. The city was populated by glamorous movie stars, famous directors, and pipe-smoking producers, who rented magnificent villas on the Via Appia Antica. It was a splendid time.

In the 1963 movie *Yesterday, Today, and Tomorrow*, directed by Vittorio De Sica, Sophia Loren plays Mara, a woman who lives in a charming apartment overlooking Piazza Navona, where she also pursues her profession—the oldest in the world. Her favorite client is Augusto, played by Marcello Mastroianni. Her neighbors regard her with suspicion, but their grandson Umberto, who is studying to become a priest, is on the verge of abandoning his vocation for her. His grandmother wants Mara to discourage him. Mara makes a vow: in return for Umberto returning to the seminary, she will not indulge in any worldly pleasures for one week. Every cloud has a silver lining.

In Italy, every occasion is worthy of a celebration. New Year's Day comes wrapped with the hopes of winning the lottery and a *cotechino* wrapped in pastry (*see* page 218); on the 6th of January, Epiphany brings stockings filled with sweets to reward children who have been good and lumps of "coal" in the form of crystallized sugar to sweetly punish the bad ones. Women are celebrated on the 8th of March with mimosa cake (*see* page 204). Easter season starts early with a pecorino cheese bread (*see* page 211), when, after the excesses of Carnival and its immoderate intake of *castagnole* (*see* page 223), people are traditionally required to renounce all animal products, the promised rewards being eternal life and an improved waistline. A summer of eating salads is interrupted by Ferragosto, signaling the importance of outdoor togetherness and the pleasures of fruits in syrup (*see* page 217).

December, with its irresistible "false fish" (*see* page 222), brings with it our desire to be good, or simply a bit better . . . until the next day, at least. Then there are birthdays, with their endless good wishes, of course. I myself much prefer celebrating unbirthdays, *Alice in Wonderland*-style. I like to find a good excuse for a celebration each and every day, and just be merry. Not for nothing am I utterly and undiplomatically Italian.

Palline ricotta e cocco

RICOTTA & COCONUT BALLS

I use confectioners' sugar for this recipe because it's much easier to combine with the rest of the ingredients, getting the preparation time for this dish down to under 10 minutes. If I were a civilized eater, I would tell you that it takes less time to make these sweet balls of coconut and ricotta than it does to eat them, and that the amount below is enough for about six people. Wait until you try them though—they are so good you will probably want to double the ingredients to satisfy any crowd larger than two.

Preparation time: 10 minutes plus chilling

Makes: about 35 small balls

Serves 2 to 6 (depending on greed)

10½oz ricotta cheese

¾ cup confectioners' sugar

2 tablespoons heavy whipping cream or light cream

2 cups desiccated coconut, divided, plus extra for dusting

In a large bowl, mix together the ricotta, sugar, cream, and two-thirds of the desiccated coconut until soft.

Put the remaining desiccated coconut in a large shallow bowl. Divide the ricotta mixture into small walnut-sized lumps and shape into balls, then roll in the desiccated coconut until evenly coated. Arrange the ricotta balls on a large serving dish, cover with plastic wrap, and let chill in the refrigerator for at least 3 hours before serving.

Mimosa al profumo di ananas con fiorellini zuccherati

PINEAPPLE-FLAVORED MIMOSA CAKE WITH CANDIED FLOWERS

In the alleys of the eternal city, you might bump into a lady carrying a basket of flowers on her head. "Would you care for a bunch of violets?" she says, and she offers you a purple bundle as she crosses herself.
On the 8th of March, women are traditionally celebrated with a bunch of mimosa blossoms and a mimosa-shaped cake. Mine is decorated with fresh and candied flowers, which you should make the day before. Be sure to prepare the spongecake base in advance, too; it needs to cool completely before you fill it. This wonderfully fresh dessert makes quite a spectacle.

Preparation time: 45 minutes plus cooling, soaking and overnight drying

Cooking time: 50 minutes

Makes 1 x 9-inch cake

6 eggs

²/₃ cup superfine sugar

1 teaspoon ground ginger

1 vanilla bean, split lengthwise and seeds scraped

pinch of salt

²/₃ cup cornstarch, sifted

²/₃ cup all-purpose flour, sifted

Custard:

3 egg yolks

3 tablespoons superfine sugar

1¹/₂ cups milk

zest of 1 lemon

3 tablespoons all-purpose flour, sifted

¹/₂ cup pineapple juice

Filling:

1¹/₄ cups heavy whipping cream

¹/₂ cup confectioners' sugar

2 cups fresh pineapple chunks, ¹/₂-inch in size

For the candied flowers, place the sugar in a small bowl. Coat one of the flowers on all sides with the egg white using a small brush, then hold it over the sugar bowl using a pair of tweezers. Gently spoon the sugar onto the flower until each petal is coated. Place the flower on a large sheet of parchment paper, then repeat with the remaining flowers. Let dry at room temperature overnight.

For the spongecake, preheat the oven to 350°F. Line a 9-inch springform cake pan with parchment paper.

Put the eggs, sugar, ginger, vanilla seeds, and salt in a bowl and mix together with a hand-held electric beater for 10 minutes until fluffy. Add the sifted cornstarch and flour and beat for another 1 to 2 minutes to form a smooth batter.

Pour the batter into the cake pan in an even layer and bake in the center of the oven for 40 minutes, until lightly golden and the center springs back when pressed lightly with your fingers. Transfer the spongecake to a wire rack to cool in the pan before turning it out.

While the spongecake is cooling, make the pineapple custard. Beat the egg yolks together with the sugar in a medium saucepan off the heat for 5 minutes until pale and fluffy. Add the milk and lemon zest and heat gently for 2 to 3 minutes, then stir in the flour and bring to a gentle simmer. Let the custard bubble away for a further 2 to 3 minutes before stirring in the pineapple juice. Continue to simmer, stirring, until the custard is thick enough to coat the back of a spoon, then pour the custard into a bowl and let cool for 30 minutes. Cover with plastic wrap and transfer to the refrigerator for 2 hours to chill.

For the syrup, put the sugar and water in a small saucepan and bring to a boil. Remove from the heat and stir in the liqueur, then let cool at room temperature for 20 minutes.

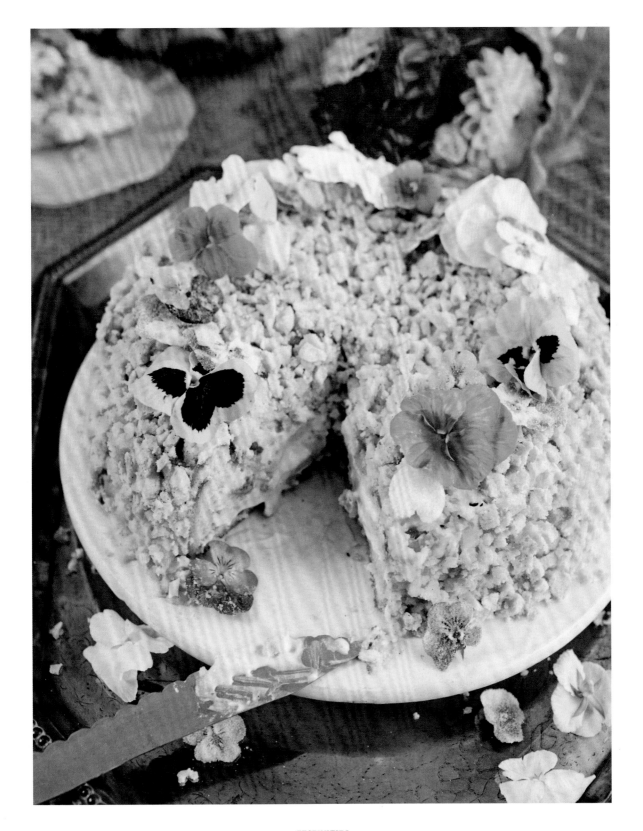

Syrup:

¼ cup superfine sugar

½ cup water

2 tablespoons rum, brandy, or
    Cognac

Candied flowers:

¼ cup superfine sugar

25 edible flowers, plus extra fresh
    flower to decorate

1 egg white, beaten

For the filling, pour the cream into a bowl and beat, adding the confectioners' sugar a tablespoon at a time, until all the sugar is incorporated and the cream is nice and fluffy. Gently fold the whipped cream into the cooled custard together with the pineapple pieces until everything is mixed together well.

To assemble the cake, carefully slice the spongecake horizontally one-third of the way up into two layers. Set the larger top layer aside, brushing the surface with a little of the syrup to lightly moisten it. With a sharp knife and a spoon, carve out a large circle in the bottom layer almost to the edges of the cake, leaving a depth of ½ inch at the bottom. Remove the carved-out spongecake from the bottom layer and cut it into ⅛-inch crumblike cubes. Set aside.

Transfer the hollowed bottom layer to a serving plate. Brush the sides and hollowed-out bottom generously with the syrup, then fill it with half the pineapple custard. Level the filling off using a spatula, then cover with the larger spongecake layer, top-side down.

Brush the top of the cake generously with the syrup, then spread the remaining pineapple custard evenly over the top and sides of the cake, pressing the cake cubes gently into the custard all over to fix them in place. Carefully cover with plastic wrap and refrigerate for at least 2 hours until the custard has set firm. Serve cold, decorated with a mixture of fresh and candied edible flowers.

Cuzzupa Pasquale

EASTER BREAD WITH EGGS

This sweet, speckled Easter bread is decorated with an egg, an ancient symbol of rebirth. To shape these breads, find a drawing of a bell online, print it out onto a sheet of letter paper, and cut it out to use as a template. Or, if you like, purchase a bell-shaped cookie cutter. These edible bell–shaped breads also make a nice Easter table decoration.

Preparation time: 20 minutes

Cooking time: 20 minutes

Makes 4 loaves

2 teaspoons baking powder

$1/3$ cup milk

4 eggs

$3/4$ cup superfine sugar

2 cups all-purpose flour, sifted

2 cups bread flour, sifted

zest of 1 lemon

$1/2$ cup vegetable oil

To decorate:

5 hard-boiled eggs

1 cup sifted confectioners' sugar

3 tablespoons milk

$1^3/4$oz colored sugar strands

Preheat the oven to 350°F. Line a cookie sheet with parchment paper.

Dissolve the baking powder in the milk in a bowl. In a separate bowl, beat the eggs and sugar together until fluffy.

Pour the egg and sugar mixture into a large mixing bowl or the bowl of an electric stand mixer fitted with the dough hook. Add the baking powder mixture, flours, lemon zest, and vegetable oil and mix together to form a firm dough.

Divide the dough into five equal-sized parts and roll each out on a lightly floured work surface into a 4 x 8-inch rectangle. Shape the trimmings into four little bells, approximately $5/8$ inch thick and arrange on top of four of the dough rectangles. Place four of the rectangles on the prepared cookie sheet and cut the final rectangle across the longest side into eight strips measuring $1/2$ inch wide.

To decorate, place an egg in the center of a bell and place two of the dough strips to form a cross over the egg and fix it in place. Repeat with the remaining rectangles.

Mix two tablespoons of boiling water together with the confectioners' sugar until smooth.

Brush all four loaves with milk and coat the crosses with the confectioners' sugar glaze. Sprinkle all over with the colored sugar strands and bake in the oven for 20 minutes until nice and golden.

Let cool on a wire rack for at least 1 hour before serving.

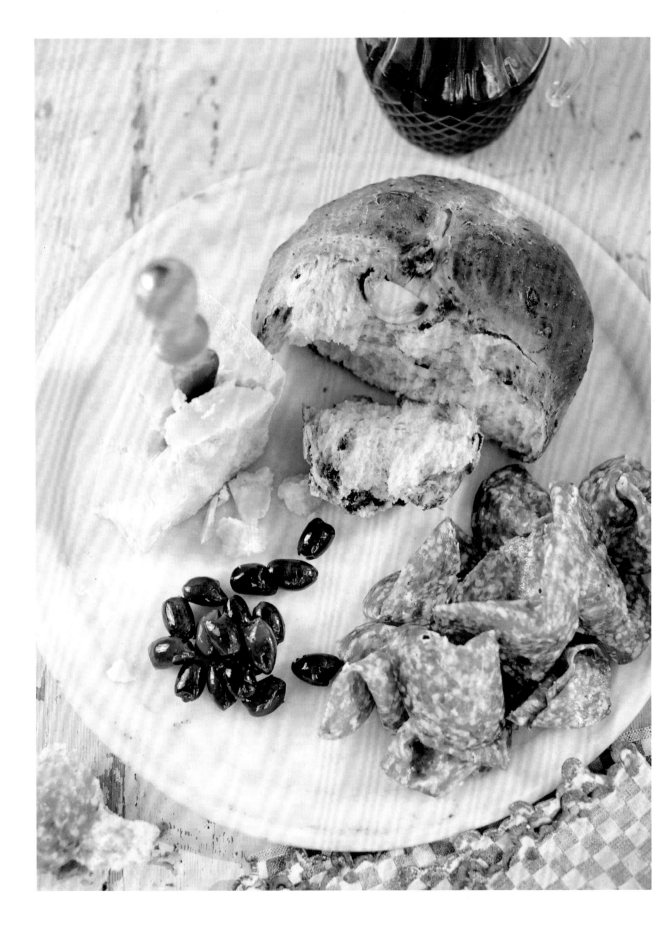

Pane di Pasqua con pecorino, miele e salame

EASTER BREAD WITH PECORINO CHEESE, HONEY & SALAMI

Breaking bread together is an ancient gesture, an act of sharing the essential joys of life. This superb puffy bread is a wonderful accompaniment for cold meats and the savory treats typical of regional Italian food, greedily consumed during the holidays as if there's no tomorrow. It's also great with soup. The proving time is quite long, giving you the opportunity to dedicate yourself to your favorite hobbies. Perfect for a rainy Sunday.

Preparation time: 15 minutes plus proving

Cooking time: 30 minutes

Makes 4 loaves

2 tablespoons fast-acting dry yeast

1 teaspoon superfine sugar

1/2 cup lukewarm water

2 1/4 lb bread flour

3 tablespoons extra virgin olive oil

7oz pecorino romano cheese, 3 1/2 oz grated and 3 1/2 oz cut into 1/2-inch cubes

1/3 cup sesame seeds

pinch of salt

5 1/2 oz whole Italian Milano salami, cut into 1/2-inch cubes

1/2 cup liquid honey

4 garlic cloves, peeled and left whole

Dissolve the yeast and sugar together in the lukewarm water.

Sift the flour into a large bowl. Make a well in the center, add the yeast mixture and the oil, and mix everything together to form a dough. Knead for 5 minutes, then add the grated pecorino, sesame seeds, and salt and continue to knead until the dough is smooth and elastic. Add the pecorino and salami pieces, ensuring they are distributed evenly throughout the dough. Cover the bowl with a damp dish cloth and let the dough stand in a warm place for 1 1/2 hours to prove.

Uncover the proven dough and, using a sharp knife, make two cuts about 1/2 inch deep into it in the shape of a cross (this will help delay the proving and develop the flavors within the loaf). Let stand to prove for another 1 1/2 hours, then cut again in the same way and let prove for a final hour until the dough is twice its original size.

Once the proving is done, add the honey to the bowl and knead it into the bread until it's fully absorbed. Divide the dough into four equal-sized pieces and shape into circular loaves, cutting a cross on top of each. Let the loaves rise again for a final 15 minutes.

Preheat the oven to 350°F. Line a cookie sheet with parchment paper.

Lightly brush the surface of the loaves with water and place a garlic clove on top of each. Transfer to the prepared cookie sheet and bake in the oven for 30 minutes, or until thoroughly golden.

Remove the loaves from the oven and transfer to a wire rack to cool for at least 30 minutes before breaking bread.

IMPERIAL-STYLE SWEET GOLDEN BREAD WITH CLEMENTINE GELATIN

This dessert is associated with the winter solstice on the 21st of December. In the days of the Roman Empire, it was prepared to increase the chances of the sun making a comeback. With my own usual zigzagging between Rome, Paris, and London, I bring you my updated version of this old-fashioned treat. Widening the horizon, and bringing it back in style. Roar!

Preparation time: 30 minutes plus chilling, soaking, and rising

Cooking time: 30 to 40 minutes

Serves 8 to 10

1/4 cup fast-acting dry yeast

3/4 cup lukewarm milk

13/4lb bread flour, divided

4 large eggs

3/4 cup superfine sugar, plus extra to decorate

1 stick unsalted butter, melted

zest of 1 lemon

Filling:

2/3 cup raisins

1/3 cup soft dried figs

1/4 cup soft dried prunes, pitted

1/3 cup blanched almonds, coarsely chopped

1/3 cup hazelnuts, coarsely chopped

1/2 cup unsalted pistachios, coarsely chopped

2/3 cup chopped walnuts

13/4oz good-quality baking chocolate (about 75% cocoa solids), very finely chopped

1/3 cup pine nuts

zest of 1 orange

1/2 stick unsalted butter

1 tablespoon bread crumbs (*see* page 262)

For the clementine gelatin, soak the gelatin leaves in a bowl filled with cold water for 10 minutes, then remove and squeeze out the excess water.

Bring the clementine juice, wine, and sugar to a simmer in a small saucepan over low heat. Remove from the heat and mix together with the gelatin leaves until melted. Pour the liquid into 8 small dessert glasses and put them in the refrigerator to cool and set for at least 4 hours.

To make the *pangiallo*, mix the yeast together with the milk in a cup until dissolved, then pour into a large bowl and mix together with 11/3 cups of the flour to form a smooth, elastic dough. Let stand to prove in a warm place for 1 hour until the dough has doubled in size.

Once the dough has proved, beat the eggs and sugar together in a separate bowl until pale and fluffy. Tip the egg mixture into the bowl of an electric stand mixer fitted with the dough hook, along with the melted butter, remaining flour, lemon zest, and proved dough and knead together to form a smooth, sticky dough. Transfer the dough to a bowl, cover with a clean dish cloth, and let rise further in a warm place for 1 hour.

Preheat the oven to 375°F.

While the dough is rising, prepare the filling. Soak the raisins, figs, and prunes in water for 10 minutes, then drain them well. Coarsely chop the figs and prunes and place them in a bowl with the raisins, chopped nuts, chocolate, pine nuts, orange zest, and raisins, stirring everything together well.

Melt the butter in a small saucepan, add the bread crumbs, and cook, stirring, for a few minutes until lightly toasted. Tip the bread crumbs into the fruit and nut mixture.

In a separate bowl, beat the egg whites together with a pinch of salt until stiff peaks form. Fold the egg whites along with the beaten yolks into the fruit mixture.

For the egg wash, beat the egg yolk together with the saffron threads in a small bowl.

3 large eggs, separated and
  yolks beaten

pinch of salt

Egg wash:

1 egg yolk

10 to 15 saffron threads

Decoration:

1 x 9³/₄-oz filo pastry sheet,
  thawed if frozen

¹/₂ cup confectioners' sugar

1 tablespoon water

Clementine gelatin:

¹/₂oz fine gelatin leaves

juice of 20 seedless clementines
  (approximately 1 cup)

1¹/₄ cups pink moscato,
  champagne, or other
  sparkling wine

2 tablespoons superfine sugar

3 tablespoons pomegranate seeds

Roll the risen dough out on a lightly floured work surface into a rectangle measuring 15 x 10¹/₂-inches. Spread the filling over the surface of the dough, leaving a ³/₄-inch border around the edges. Then, starting from one of the longer sides, roll up the dough to form a long sausage. Starting with one end, roll up the sausage into a spiral shape, then gently transfer it to a cookie sheet. Brush the surface with the egg wash and sprinkle with a little extra sugar.

Bake in the oven for 30 to 40 minutes until golden brown, then transfer to a wire rack to cool.

While the *pangiallo* is cooling, make the decoration. Unroll the filo pastry sheet and cut out about 50 to 60 star shapes in three different sizes, either using cookie cutters or freestyle, using a small sharp knife. Arrange the pastry stars on a cookie sheet covered with parchment paper (you can brush them with melted butter if you like a crispy effect) and bake for 3 to 5 minutes until golden, then transfer to a wire rack to cool.

In a small pan, gently heat the water together with the confectioners' sugar until dissolved, then stir until creamy.

Overlay three stars of different sizes and glue them together with a drop of the confectioners' sugar glaze, then use a little more glaze to attach them to the *pangiallo*. Repeat with the remaining stars until the entire snail is covered.

When ready to serve, remove the clementine gelatin from the refrigerator and scatter with the pomegranate seeds. Serve alongside the *pangiallo*, cut into thick slices.

Pesche sciroppate con panna

POACHED PEACHES IN SYRUP WITH CREAM

Ferragosto is a public holiday in Italy, celebrated on the 15th of August, which is also the Feast of the Assumption. All the major cities are deserted as people take a celebratory *gita fuori porta*—literally an excursion outside the city walls. Forget about packing a small picnic to eat under the shade of a tree; no, for an Italian family this means full-on cutlery, cake, and pans of lasagne. At the end of the meal you'll be spoonfed—and I don't mean this figuratively— poached fruit in honeyed syrup. You've just earned yourself a digestif and a nap under the tree. The peaches here need to be stored for a minimum of 15 days before using in order to develop their beautiful flavors, and will keep for up to six months. You could also enjoy these peaches with prosciutto, instead of the usual melon.

Preparation time: 15 minutes plus storing

Cooking time: 35 minutes

Makes 4 x 9fl-oz jars

2¼ lb yellow or white peaches

¼ cup lemon juice

4 cups water

1½ cups superfine sugar

12 cloves

4 cinnamon sticks

4 star anise

4 vanilla beans

To serve (enough for 4):

1¼ cups heavy whipping cream

small handful of mint leaves (optional)

⅔ cup blackberries (optional)

Peel, stone, and quarter the peaches, placing the peach pieces in a large bowl of water together with the lemon juice as you go to prevent them from darkening.

Fill a large Dutch oven with water and bring it to a boil. Carefully lower the peach quarters into the boiling water and blanch for 2 minutes, then drain the peaches and hold them under cold running water to cool.

Once cool, fill the jars with the peach quarters, leaving at a gap of at least ½ inch between the top of the peaches and the top of each jar.

Pour the measured water and sugar into a heavy saucepan. Bring to a boil, then lower the heat and simmer for 2 to 3 minutes to form a thick, transparent syrup. Remove from the heat.

Pour the syrup over the peaches to cover completely. Divide the cloves, cinnamon, star anise, and vanilla beans between the jars and screw on the lids tightly. Invert the jars and let cool to room temperature.

Once the jars have cooled, place them in the center of a large saucepan. Tie the jars together with a clean dish cloth (this will prevent them from moving around and chipping), cover them with water, and bring to a boil. Boil for 30 minutes, then turn off the heat and let the jars cool in the pan for a further 30 minutes before removing from the water and drying. Store the jars in a cool, dry place away from sunlight for a minimum of 15 days before using to allow the flavors to fully develop.

When you are ready to enjoy a jar of the peaches, whip the cream until stiff.

Transfer the peaches and a little of their syrup juice into a serving bowl, spoon some whipped cream on top, and scatter with some mint leaves and blackberries to finish, if you like.

Cotechino in crosta con insalata di finocchi, olive, arance e melograno

CRUSTED COTECHINO
WITH FENNEL, OLIVE, ORANGE
& POMEGRANATE SALAD

Here I'm paying homage to the British beef Wellington with my Anglo-Italian version of a classic New Year's Eve combination: lentils and *cotechino*, both symbols of abundant good wishes for the year ahead. You can find *cotechino* sausage in most Italian delis, but if you don't want to make the trip, there are also many online suppliers that sell it. Slices of *cotechino* prepared in this way are also delicious dipped in Red Onion Preserve (*see* page 263).

Preparation time: 25 minutes plus cooling

Cooking time: 1½ hours

Serves 6

1lb 2oz precooked *cotechino* sausage

1 small carrot, finely chopped

1 shallot, finely chopped

1 celery stalk, trimmed and finely chopped

small handful of dill fronds, finely chopped

1 rosemary sprig, leaves picked and finely chopped

¼ cup extra virgin oil

¾ cup dried brown lentils

¾oz dried porcini mushrooms (ceps), soaked in 1¼ cups boiling water for at least 10 minutes

1 x 11½-oz shortcrust pastry sheet, thawed if frozen

1 teaspoon heavy whipping cream, light cream, or milk

1 large egg yolk

salt and pepper

Prepare the *cotechino* following the package directions or by cooking it in its aluminum wrapping in a large Dutch oven of boiling water for 20 to 30 minutes. Remove the *cotechino* from the water with a slotted spoon, let it cool for at least 10 minutes, then extract it from its wrapping. Discard the jelly skin coating the meat and set the *cotechino* aside in a dish.

Preheat the oven to 350°F. Line a baking pan with parchment paper.

Meanwhile, prepare a *soffritto* by sweating the chopped carrot, shallot, celery, and herbs together with the oil in a pan over low heat for 10 minutes. Add the lentils along with the porcini mushrooms and their soaking liquid, bring to a simmer, and cook gently for 30 to 40 minutes until the lentils are soft but retain a little bite. Season with salt and pepper, then tip the mixture into a food processor and blend to a coarse paste. Set aside.

Carefully roll out the pastry sheet and lay it in the center of the lined baking pan. Place the *cotechino* in the middle of the pastry sheet, spoon the lentil paste evenly over it to cover, and roll the pastry around the sausage to form a tight log. Seal the edges of the pastry, cutting off any excess (you can use this to make decorative shapes to cover the pastry crust—I love to make leaves).

Mix the cream and egg yolk together to make a wash and use it brush all over the surface of the pastry. Bake the *cotechino* in the oven for 30 minutes until the pastry crust is golden.

While the *cotechino* is cooking, prepare the salad. Soak the raisins in a small bowl filled with water for 10 minutes. Drain and set aside.

Squeeze one of the oranges and strain the juice. With a sharp knife, remove and discard the peel from the remaining orange and cut the orange flesh into ½-inch slices.

Salad:

3¹/₂ tablespoons raisins

2 oranges

6oz baby Belgian endives

1 fennel bulb

³/₄ cup black olives, pitted

¹/₂ cup pomegranate seeds

¹/₄ cup pine nuts

¹/₄ cup walnut pieces

3 tablespoons extra virgin olive oil

pinch of salt

Trim and thinly slice the baby Belgian endives and the fennel bulb, setting aside the leafy fennel fronds, and arrange the slices in a salad bowl together with the orange slices, olives, pomegranate seeds, pine nuts, walnut pieces, and raisins.

Finely chop the fennel fronds and combine with the oil, orange juice, and salt to make a dressing. Toss the salad in the dressing to coat before serving with the pastry-wrapped *cotechino*, cut into ⁵/₈-inch slices.

Pesce finto di Natale

CHRISTMAS "FISH"

Not far from the Pantheon stands Sant'Ignazio Church, built in the grand Baroque style. When I walk past its massive Corinthian pilasters I think I'm seeing double; I am mesmerized by the richly adorned altar and stare up at the cupola—it looks as if a bright blue sky is awaiting me outside. I can't believe my eyes, but then again I shouldn't. The cupola is a *trompe l'œil* painting. It's a trick of the eye. So too is this festive dish—a fake Christmas "fish" that is fun to make with kids. If you have a suitable fish mold, so much the better. Alternatively, you can shape it according to your own taste. Make it spectacularly Roman or make it all yours.

Preparation time: 10 minutes plus chilling

Cooking time: 20 minutes

Serves 8

2¼lb round red or round white potatoes, peeled and cut into ½-inch cubes

1lb 2oz canned tuna in springwater

8 anchovy fillets in olive oil, drained

¾ cup pitted green olives, plus 1 extra to garnish

2 teaspoons dried oregano

½ stick unsalted butter, softened

1 teaspoon capers in vinegar, drained

zest of 1 lemon

1 medium cucumber, cut into ¼-inch disks

1 medium carrot, cut into ¼-inch disks

1 cup mayonnaise

salt

Bring a saucepan of salted water to a boil. Add the potatoes, cover, and simmer over medium–high heat for 20 minutes, or until the potatoes are entirely soft.

Meanwhile, put the tuna, anchovies, olives, oregano, butter, and capers in a food processor and blend together to a thick, creamy paste. Stir in the lemon zest and set aside.

Drain the potato pieces, tip them into a large bowl, and coarsely mash them with a fork. Add the tuna paste and mix everything together well.

Spoon the tuna and potato mixture into a fish mold and turn it out onto the center of a large serving plate. Alternatively, spoon the mixture into the center of the plate and sculpt it into a fish shape using your hands.

Arrange the cucumber and carrot slices over the "fish" like scales and add an olive as an eye, then use a spatula to coat the surface evenly with the mayonnaise.

Transfer to the refrigerator and let chill for at least 1 hour before serving.

Castagnole di carnevale alla Romana

ROMAN-STYLE CARNIVAL SWEET DOUGH BALLS

In the musical *Rugantino*, the title character asks the city of Rome itself to be his partner in crime as he tries to seduce a married woman. *"Sceji tutte le stelle più brillarelle che c'hai, e un friccico de luna tutta pè noi."* "Light up all your bright stars, and a glimmer of moonlight just for us." But then again, everyone allows themselves transgressions during Carnival, a time when people from all walks of life would traditionally cross each other's paths, a *castagnola* in their hand as a matchmaker. Nine months later, the nuns would find a basket with a newborn on their doorstep. Here, I chart my love for uncompromised gluttonous pleasures.

Preparation time: 10 minutes

Cooking time: 15 minutes

Makes 30 *castagnole*

2 eggs

1 cup all-purpose flour

⅓ cup cornstarch

1 vanilla bean, split lengthwise and seeds scraped

zest of 1 lemon

1 teaspoon baking powder

2 tablespoons extra virgin olive oil

½ cup confectioners' sugar, plus extra for dusting

1 tablespoon Roman-Style Sambuca (*see* page 271), Marsala, or sherry

pinch of salt

Preheat the oven to 350°F. Line a cookie sheet with parchment paper.

Beat the eggs together in a large bowl until fluffy. Sift in the flour, add the cornstarch, vanilla seeds, lemon zest, baking powder, oil, confectioners' sugar, and liqueur and mix everything together thoroughly to form a smooth, sticky dough. Add the salt, cover with a clean dish cloth, and let the dough rest for 5 minutes.

Once rested, roll the dough out on a lightly floured work surface into a long sausage shape. Slice the dough sausage into 1-inch pieces and shape each into a hazelnut-sized ball.

Arrange the dough balls on the prepared cookie sheet, leaving about ½ inch of space between each, and bake for 15 minutes until the *castagnole* have risen by about one-third and are lightly golden. Transfer to a wire rack and let cool for 10 minutes.

Once cool, arrange the *castagnole* on a serving dish in a pyramid shape before dusting them with a coating of confectioners' sugar to finish.

Chapter 9
CAKES & CO.

Separated from Rome's historical center by a bridge, Trastevere is a different world: artists, artisans, and intellectuals populate a district where religious processions alternate with gay pride marches and food festivals. The fountain of Piazza Trilussa was moved here from the other side of the river in an act of cultural munificence—a present to a part of town that, in comparison with the rest, had little in the way of monuments.

The Grand Tour exposed the offspring of wealthy families to the cultural legacy of Rome. More often than not, at night these young men would venture into the city's less savory districts, of which Trastevere was one, to play cards and gamble. If a cheat was discovered, the police were called and the guilty party would spend the night in a cell—or *al fresco*, as the Romans say.

For a long time, my favorite spot in Trastevere was a *pasticceria* that had been there for almost 100 years. Virginia, the lady who welcomed me to this little *confetteria*, embodied the essence of the Roman *matrona*: a rather imposing woman, in charge of the family. She always made sure I ate enough, and offered me her beloved son's latest gastronomic creations. When she first told me about him, I imagined a young boy working wonders at the back of the shop. When she finally introduced me to this supposed child prodigy of baking, I found myself, much to my surprise, staring up at a guy of about six foot five.

The walls of the shop were covered with this man's surreal paintings, each resolving one of the many Roman historical dilemmas, the same ones one could often observe being fiercely debated just outside the *pasticceria*. I was always open to the eccentric points of view provided by Virginia on various topics, a fork in her hand to emphatically make her point and a piece of Grandma's Custard Pie (*see* page 238) on her hand-painted china plate, from the protests of 1968 to the separation of church and state. Sadly, this historic place closed in May 2015, due to the sudden deaths of both signora Virginia and her son. They left in gentle silence and with the scent of chocolate slowly fading away. I am left with memories of a miniature of Rome painted by the scrupulous hand of a talented mommy's boy, who made the best Castagnaccio (*see* page 245) in town. *Laudemus tortam.*

Fruttini gelato

ICE CREAM FRUITS

Here is a scrumptious dessert you can indulge in without having to loosen your belt. I love to get these perfumed morsels—nothing more than fruity ice cream served in the fruit's own frozen skin—out of the freezer at the end of an impromptu dinner. All you need to do is remove the flesh of the fruit and then freeze its shell, which will serve as the vessel for the fruity ice cream itself. Serve them in a bowl as if they were simply fruit—your friends will be amazed to find the ice cream surprise inside!

Preparation time: 40 minutes plus freezing

Serves 8

4 figs

4 small pears

12 large cherries or
    12 blackberries plus a handful of
    blackberries for the filling

1 pint vanilla ice cream

3 tablespoons heavy whipping
    cream

small handful of mint leaves

Start off by preparing the fruits. Cut the figs and pears into halves and very gently excavate the flesh with the help of a teaspoon, setting the flesh aside in separate bowls. Repeat the same process with the cherries, if using, placing the flesh in a separate bowl and taking off the stalks and removing the pits as you go. Cut 12 blackberries, if using, into halves and set aside. Place the remaining handful of blackberries in a separate bowl and blitz them together.

Place the fruit "shells" in a dish and transfer to the freezer for 2 hours until frozen solid.

Add one-third of the ice cream along with a tablespoon of heavy whipping cream, if using, to each of the fruit bowls. Mix together well to give you three different kinds of fruit-flavored ice cream.

Remove the fruit "shells" from the freezer one type of fruit at a time. Fill the halves of each fruit with their respective ice cream, then sandwich them together to make them whole again. Return to the freezer for at least 30 minutes, or until needed.

To serve, arrange the frozen fruits in a fruit bowl and decorate with the mint leaves.

Meringona alla Romana con salsa di arance

ROMAN-STYLE MERINGUE WITH ORANGE SAUCE

There's the cotton candy sold on Piazza Navona as Christmas approaches, and then there's the much more civilized Roman meringue. Romans make enormous meringues, reaching almost impossible heights. Why? Because once the Romans actually get around to doing, they often overdo. The secret to making a successful meringue is to make sure to add your sugar a little at a time and keep whisking. Cloud-shaped Roman megalomania.

Preparation time: 15 minutes

Cooking time: 1 hour 15 minutes plus cooling

Serves 6

1¼ cups confectioners' sugar

⅔ cup superfine sugar

6 extra-large egg whites

pinch of salt

1 tablespoon cornstarch

Orange sauce:

juice of 4 oranges

¼ cup confectioners' sugar

2 tablespoons orange blossom
  water

To serve:

1¼ cups heavy whipping cream

2 tablespoons chopped mint leaves

2 tablespoons rose petals or edible
  red glitter

Preheat the oven to 300°F. Line a cookie sheet with parchment paper.

Combine the two sugars in a small bowl.

Put the egg whites in a large bowl with a pinch of salt. Beat the egg whites together, adding the cornstarch after a few minutes, until they form stiff peaks. Keep beating vigorously and start adding the sugar mixture a tablespoon at a time (it's imperative to add the sugar gradually—no one wants a watery meringue) until the mixture is glossy and thick.

With the help of a spatula or 2 large spoons, form six billowy meringues on the prepared cookie sheet, gently flicking the spatula or spoon as you deposit the mixture on the cookie sheet to give the meringues a pointed, spiky finish.

Bake the meringues for 1 hour until pale and creamy in color, then switch off the oven, open the door slightly, and let the meringues cool in the oven for 15 minutes.

While the meringues are cooling, make the orange sauce. Pour the orange juice into a small saucepan, add the confectioners' sugar and orange blossom water, and bring to a boil. Lower the heat and let simmer for 5 minutes, until the sauce is syrupy and smooth.

To serve, whip the cream until stiff and stir in the chopped mint. Divide the cream between individual serving plates, spooning it into the center of each plate. Place the meringues on top of the cream and spoon the sauce over them, finishing each plate with a scattering of rose petals or edible glitter.

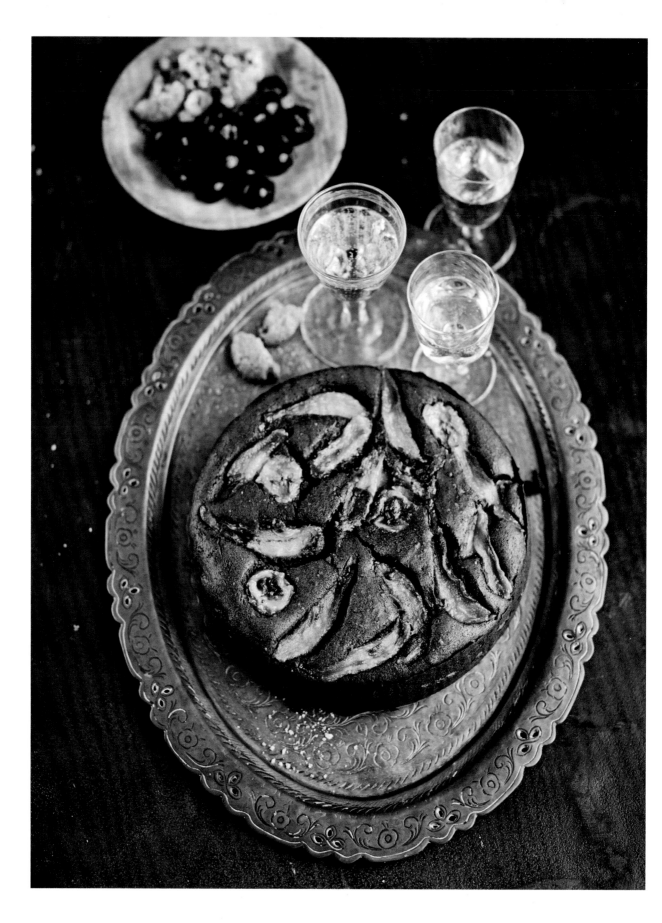

Torta al cioccolato, amaretti e tutti frutti

CHOCOLATE, AMARETTI & TUTTI FRUTTI CAKE

One day, as I was eating my chocolate cake in a tiny family-run restaurant in Rome, I saw a large group of people happily eating, drinking, and being merry. Then they started leaving one by one, trying to go unnoticed. Eventually, only the man at the head of the table remained. The waiter went up to him, only to hear this fateful sentence: "May I come by tomorrow to settle *la dolorosa*?" ("The painful one"—an Italian synonym for the bill.) "No, *dotto*" (all Roman restaurateurs address their clientele as "doctor"), "either you pay now or I will kick your ass." Sometimes, eating at home is so much safer. Roman faces, *tutti frutti*.

Preparation time: 20 minutes

Cooking time: 1 hour

Serves 8

7oz good-quality baking chocolate (about 70% cocoa solids), coarsely chopped

1¾ sticks unsalted butter, divided

pinch of salt

1½ cups rum

4 pears, peeled, cored, and cut into wedges

1 large banana, sliced

⅔ cup light brown sugar

4 large eggs, separated

1 tablespoon baking powder

½ cup lukewarm milk

1 cup amaretti cookie crumbs

1 tablespoon chopped thyme leaves, fresh or dried

1⅔ cups all-purpose flour, sifted

¾ cup pitted black cherries in syrup

Preheat the oven to 400°F. Line the bottom and sides of a 8½-inch springform cake pan with parchment paper.

Melt the chocolate pieces together with half the butter and a pinch of salt in a bowl set over a saucepan of lightly simmering water or in a microwave. Let cool.

Place a large nonstick skillet over high heat, add the rum and pear wedges, and cook for 10 to 15 minutes, adding the banana slices halfway through cooking and turning them over occasionally, until the liquid has evaporated and the fruit is golden and caramelized. Set aside.

In a large bowl, beat half the sugar together with the egg yolks until pale, creamy, and doubled in volume. Dissolve the baking powder in the milk and add to the bowl along with the melted chocolate, remaining butter, amaretti crumbs, thyme, and flour, stirring everything together to form a batter.

In a separate bowl, beat together the egg whites with a pinch of salt for 5 minutes until they form stiff peaks. Beating all the while, gradually add the remaining sugar, a tablespoon at a time, until the mixture is glossy and thick. Gently fold the egg-white mixture into the batter with a spatula.

Pour half the batter into the prepared pan. Spread the caramelized fruit mixture evenly over the batter, then cover the fruit mixture with the remaining batter.

Bake in the oven for 10 minutes, then lower the heat to 340°F and bake for a further 50 minutes until the surface is cracked and a toothpick or cake tester inserted into the center of the cake comes out clean. Remove the cake from the oven and transfer to a wire rack to cool for 30 minutes before turning the cake out onto a serving plate. Spoon the syrupy black cherries evenly over the surface of the cake before serving.

Semifreddo ai cantucci e Vin Santo

ALMOND COOKIE & SWEET WINE SEMIFREDDO

This dense, crumbly dessert is halfway between sorbet and gelato, but without the fuss of using a special ice-cream machine, ice cubes, and all that jazz. A dessert as fluffy as the Roman clouds when they gather spectacularly, accompanied by swooping flocks of starlings. You can catch sight of this aerial display around mid-October, as the leaves start to fall and fill the tree-lined streets of this endearing city. As an alternative to the crunchy almond *cantucci*, you can also use graham crackers, combined with a handful of hazelnuts toasted for a few minutes in a small skillet.

Preparation time: 30 minutes plus freezing

Serves 8

3 large eggs, separated

$1/4$ cup sugar

pinch of fine salt

$1^3/4$ cups heavy whipping cream

1 tablespoon lemon juice

14oz cantucci cookies, crushed, divided

$1/2$ cup Vin Santo, Marsala, or Madeira

1 cup blackberries (optional), fresh or frozen

Line a 2-pound loaf pan (measuring $9^1/2$ x $5^1/2$ x $2^1/2$ inches) with plastic wrap, allowing it to overhang the sides (this will make it easy to remove the semifreddo from the pan when it's ready).

In a large bowl, beat the egg yolks with the sugar until the mixture is pale, creamy, and almost doubled in size. In a second bowl, beat together the egg whites with a pinch of salt until stiff peaks form. In a third bowl, whip the cream until soft peaks form.

Add the egg whites to the sugar and egg yolks, then add the whipped cream, folding gently from top to bottom. Gently fold the lemon juice and one-quarter of the crushed cookies into the creamy mixture.

Tip the remaining crushed cookies into a small bowl, pour the Vin Santo over them, and mix together well.

Fill the prepared pan first with a layer of the soaked crushed cookies, then a layer of the creamy mixture. Keep alternating these layers, making sure to finish off with a layer of *cantucci*, until all the ingredients are used, then transfer to the freezer for at least 4 hours to freeze until firm.

Take the semifreddo out of the freezer 10 to 15 minutes before serving to allow it to soften slightly. When ready to serve, flip the pan upside down and turn the semifreddo out onto an oval dish. Decorate with the blackberries, if using, and cut into thick slices to serve.

Torta della nonna

GRANDMA'S CUSTARD PIE

When I was 13 or 14, I started spending all my non-school hours in the kitchen—my great-grandmother's sanctuary, which I had been forbidden to enter until then, as no messy children were allowed. I felt drawn to the mysterious calm this special room infused me with. From my family I inherited a recipe book filled with secrets that I started studying. On rainy days, I loved to chase away the gloom by putting my hands in some sweet dough. What I love about kneading dough is that you're bringing your body heat to work with the gluten and the flour: a real collaboration between you and the food. Just as my granny taught me by example and involvement, drawing me into the kitchen. From then on, I never wanted to be anywhere else. *La torta della nonna* is one of the most heart-warming and easiest cakes in the Roman baking repertoire. I've added my own twist in the form of white chocolate, for extra depth of flavor.

Preparation time: 15 minutes plus resting

Cooking time: 40 minutes

Serves 8

3$1/4$ cups all-purpose flour

2 sticks unsalted butter, chilled and cut into $1/2$-inch cubes, plus extra for greasing

pinch of salt

$3/4$ cup superfine sugar

4 egg yolks

zest of 1 lemon

$1/3$ cup pine nuts

$1/2$ cup confectioners' sugar

1oz white chocolate, to decorate

Custard:

4 egg yolks

$1/2$ cup all-purpose flour

2 cups milk

$1/2$ cup superfine sugar

zest of 1 lemon

1$3/4$oz white chocolate, broken into chips

For the custard, whisk together the egg yolks, flour, milk, sugar, and lemon zest in a saucepan. Heat gently, stirring continuously, for 10 minutes over low heat, or until the custard is thick enough to coat the back of a spoon. Stir the white chocolate into the hot custard to melt and mix together well. Remove from the heat and set aside to cool.

Place the flour in a bowl, add the butter and salt, and rub in with the fingertips until the mixture resembles coarse bread crumbs. Form a well in the center and pour in the sugar, egg yolks, and lemon zest. Mix everything together by hand briefly to form a smooth pastry dough (try to avoid working the pastry for too long, otherwise you'll melt the butter, and no one wants a soggy pastry). Seal the dough in plastic wrap, transfer to the refrigerator, and let rest for 30 minutes.

Preheat the oven to 350°F. Grease a 9-inch pie plate with butter.

Once rested, divide the dough into two equal-sized pieces. On a floured work surface, roll each dough piece into a 10-inch circle using a rolling pin. Line the bottom and inside of the prepared pie plate with one of the dough circles, pressing it down gently to fix it in place. Trim off any excess.

Pour the custard into the pastry shell, cover it with the second pastry circle, and pinch the edges together using your fingers to seal the pie, trimming off the excess pastry as necessary. Scatter with the pine nuts and dust with the confectioners' sugar, then bake in the oven for 30 minutes until the pastry is golden and the pine nuts are well toasted.

Remove the pie from the oven, transfer to a wire rack, and let cool for 1 hour. Grate some white chocolate onto the pie to decorate, then serve.

Crostata ricotta e cioccolato come al ghetto

GHETTO-STYLE RICOTTA & CHOCOLATE PIE

The ruins of the Roman Forum encompass the various eras of Rome—there are temples, the Christian basilica of Santa Francesca Romana, the remnants of triumphal arches, and the Colosseum in the background. And then there is *crostata ricotta e cioccolato*, one of Rome's hidden splendors. Just steps from the Teatro Marcello, tucked away on the corner of the road leading to Portico d'Ottavia, the center of Rome's Jewish Ghetto, there's a *forno* that is famous for its ricotta and chocolate pie. This eternal city is a collection of different cities, one inside the other, and this recipe is a collection of flavors inside a golden pastry shell.

Preparation time: 15 minutes plus resting

Cooking time: 45 minutes

Serves 6

walnut-sized lump of unsalted butter, for greasing

1 egg yolk, beaten, for brushing

14oz ricotta

$1/4$ cup superfine sugar

zest of 1 lemon

1oz dark chocolate flakes or 1oz baking chocolate, coarsely grated

Pastry:

2 eggs

1 cup confectioners' sugar

$1/3$ cup sunflower oil

1 teaspoon baking powder

$1^1/3$ cups spelt flour, sifted

2 cups all-purpose flour, sifted

$3^1/2$ tablespoons black sesame seeds

Grease an 8-inch pie plate with butter.

For the pastry, mix the eggs together with the confectioners' sugar, oil, and baking powder in a large mixing bowl or the bowl of an electric stand mixer fitted with the dough hook. Add the sifted flours and sesame seeds and mix together briefly to form a delicate, wet dough.

Take one third of the pastry dough and wrap it in aluminum foil. Press small walnut-sized balls of the remaining pastry into the pie plate to cover the bottom and the sides. Transfer both the pan and the foil-wrapped pastry to the refrigerator to rest for 30 minutes.

Preheat the oven to 340°F.

Once rested, cover the pie shell with parchment paper and fill with dried beans. Bake blind for 20 minutes. Remove the pie plate from the oven, tip out the beans, and remove the paper. Brush the pastry with the beaten egg yolk and bake for a further 2 to 3 minutes, until lightly golden. Remove from the oven and let cool for 15 minutes.

Increase the oven temperature to 350°F.

Beat together the ricotta, sugar, and lemon zest in a bowl or mix a food processor until smooth and creamy. Fold in the chocolate flakes, then pour the chocolate and ricotta mixture into the cooled pie shell and level the filling with the back of a spoon.

Take the reserved chilled pastry out of the refrigerator and crumble it into small pieces with your fingertips. Scatter the pastry crumbs evenly over the surface of the pie and bake in the oven for 20 minutes, until the ricotta filling is firm and slightly cracked and the pastry crumbs are golden. Transfer to a wire rack to cool before enjoying at any time of day (or night).

Tiramisù al limone

LEMON TIRAMISÙ

There's nothing like giving a makeover to a classic dish—tradition with a twist. After all, in order to survive, traditions need to suit the modern sensibilities of those who still follow them. Tiramisù literally means "pick-me-up" and this dessert is all about reveling in the joys of the kitchen. If you have time, make some homemade mascarpone: you'll need a food thermometer and 24 hours' patience. Caution: this could become addictive. Don't say I didn't warn you.

Preparation time: 15 minutes plus chilling

Cooking time: 15 minutes for the mascarpone

Serves 6

6 large egg yolks

⅓ cup superfine sugar

1lb 2oz mascarpone cheese, store-bought or homemade (*see* below)

zest and juice of 1 lemon

1 tablespoon limoncello liqueur

1¼ cups whole or semiskim milk

9oz Dunking Biscotti (*see* page 32) or ladyfingers

⅔ cup unsalted pistachios

9oz mixed berries and currants, to decorate

Homemade mascarpone:

4 cups heavy whipping cream

2 tablespoons lemon juice

For the homemade mascarpone, pour the cream into a saucepan over low heat and bring to a temperature of 185°F, whisking all the while. Once the desired temperature has been reached, gradually add the lemon juice, whisking continuously, and continue to whisk for a further 5 minutes, or until the cream has thickened enough to coat the back of a spoon. Remove from the heat and let cool for 15 minutes.

Line a colander with cheesecloth and suspend over a bowl. Pour in the thickened cream and let rest at room temperature for 1 hour, then transfer the colander and bowl to the refrigerator and let chill for 24 hours. Spoon the mascarpone into an airtight container and seal until ready to use (it will keep for up to 3 to 4 days in the refrigerator).

To make the tiramisù, beat the egg yolks together with the sugar in a bowl until pale and creamy. Add the mascarpone and mix together well, then stir in the lemon juice, zest, and limoncello.

Pour the milk into a shallow bowl. Briefly dunk the biscotti in the milk for no more than a second per side (you want them to absorb a little of the liquid but still be firm). Line the bottom of a large oval dish with a layer of the milk-soaked biscotti and cover with a layer of the mascarpone mixture. Continue to layer in this fashion, finishing with a final layer of cream.

Cover the tiramisù carefully with plastic wrap and transfer to the refrigerator for at least 1 hour to chill and set. Blend the pistachios in a food processor or spice grinder to a fine powder and scatter it over the tiramisù along with the mixed berries before serving.

Torta di castagne e mele con farina alle nocciole
e arance candite

APPLE, CHESTNUT & HAZELNUT CAKE WITH CANDIED ORANGES

Roman fashion never goes out of style. World-famous designers have carved their signatures all over the city by staging their fashion shows in breathtaking settings, from the courtyards of private palazzos to the Spanish Steps. Today, those fashion entrepreneurs who cherish their city are donating funds to help preserve such historical monuments as the Colosseum. Times change and so do methods, with a common intent: to radiate splendor. You'll enjoy this cake, which mixes flavors and textures, like a stroll along Via Condotti.

Preparation time: 15 minutes

Cooking time: 1 hour 40 minutes

Serves 8

walnut-sized lump of unsalted butter, for greasing

1¼ cups all-purpose flour, plus extra for dusting

peeled zest of 1 large orange, cut into ½-inch strips

2 cooking apples

1 tablespoon lemon juice

½ cup Marsala wine

½ cup light brown sugar, divided

1½ cups hazelnuts

3 large eggs

⅔ cup superfine sugar

⅓ cup extra virgin olive oil

2 tablespoons baking powder

½ cup lukewarm milk

3½oz canned whole chestnuts, coarsely chopped

Preheat the oven to 400°F. Grease a 9-inch cake pan with butter and dust with flour.

Place the orange zest slices in a saucepan and cover with cold water. Place over high heat and bring to a boil, then drain. Repeat this process twice more, then remove the orange zest from the pan.

Peel and core the two apples. Cut one of the apples lengthwise into quarters and then each of the quarters into thin crescent-shaped slices. Place the apple slices in a bowl of water together with the lemon juice to prevent them from browning. Cut the other apple into ½-inch cubes.

Put the apple cubes into a small nonstick skillet along with the wine and two-thirds of the brown sugar. Gently heat, stirring, for 10 minutes, until the apple pieces have softened but still retain their shape. Remove from the heat and set aside.

Blend the hazelnuts in a food processor to a fine powder.

Beat the eggs together with the superfine sugar in a large bowl for 3 minutes until light and fluffy. Sift in the flour and hazelnut powder and mix together well, gradually adding the olive oil as you go. Dissolve the baking powder in the milk and add to the bowl along with the apples and chestnuts, stirring everything together to form a thick, smooth batter.

Pour the batter into the prepared cake pan, then carefully arrange the apple slices in a circular pattern on the surface. Scatter with the orange zest slices and sprinkle with the remaining brown sugar.

Bake in the oven for 10 minutes, then lower the temperature to 340°F, and bake for a further 50 minutes, until the apple slices are golden and a skewer or toothpick inserted into the center of the cake comes out clean. Let cool in the pan on a wire rack for at least 30 minutes before removing the cake from the pan and serving. Enjoy with a cup of tea.

Castagnaccio

CHESTNUT FLOUR CAKE

One of the main street foods of Rome is *caldarrosta*, roast chestnuts, which never go out of fashion. You see the vendors keeping warm by their grills on street corners, with a cup of sweet wine in one hand and a piping hot roast chestnut in the other. While this is not a recipe for roast chestnuts, it does feature the same shiny brown nut as its protagonist. Best of all, it has a curiously romantic story. Traditionally, rosemary leaves were added to the cake as a love potion: the boy who ate a slice offered to him by a girl would immediately fall in love with her and consequently marry her.
This cake is made with chestnut flour, which can be found in specialty gourmet delis (or you can buy it online) and will keep in a sealed airtight container for up to 3 days.

Preparation time: 10 minutes

Cooking time: 1 hour

Serves 6

⅓ cup extra virgin olive oil, plus extra for greasing

3 eggs

¾ cup superfine sugar

2¼ cups chestnut flour

1⅔ cups all-purpose flour

2 teaspoons baking powder

1¾ cups lukewarm milk

¼ cup unsweetened cocoa powder

1 vanilla bean, split lengthwise and seeds scraped

3 rosemary sprigs, leaves picked, divided

⅓ cup pine nuts, divided

⅓ cup raisins, soaked in warm water for 10 minutes and drained

3 tablespoons fennel seeds

2½ tablespoons pumpkin seeds

3½ tablespoons confectioners' sugar

Preheat the oven to 350°F. Grease an 8-inch cake pan with a little olive oil.

Beat the eggs and sugar together in a bowl with an electric hand mixer for 5 minutes or until light and fluffy.

Sift in the flours and baking powder, then stir them into the egg mixture along with the milk, cocoa powder, olive oil, and vanilla seeds to form a batter. Add the rosemary leaves and pine nuts, reserving a small handful of each, along with the raisins, fennel seeds, and pumpkin seeds. Stir everything together well.

Pour the batter into the prepared cake pan. Scatter with the reserved rosemary leaves and pine nuts and bake for 1 hour, or until the cake is cracked on the surface, a skewer or toothpick inserted into the center comes out clean, and the pine nuts are golden brown.

Dust with confectioners' sugar and serve warm or cold.

Rotolo ricotta e visciole

SOUR CHERRY & RICOTTA ROLL CAKE

Some varieties of sweet cherry need help with pollination, and every spring, that is the role that sour cherries play in nature. *Ricotta di pecora* (sheep-milk ricotta) has long been a great resource of the countryside around Rome, a region that used to contain more sheep than people. In 1817 Pope Pius VII used a document called a *motu proprio*, which means "on his own impulse," to extend the boundaries of the municipality of Rome, giving these under-populated territories new recognition.

I created this recipe on the occasion of a blog exchange with Elizabeth Minett, of *Haut Appétit*. In the same way, if you can forgive the blasphemy, I give new recognition to this ancient combination of ingredients—a feast for the eye and the stomach, as if by papal decree.

Preparation time: 15 minutes

Cooking time: 15 minutes

Serves 6

4 eggs, plus 1 yolk

1/2 cup superfine sugar

2 tablespoons unsweetened cocoa powder

1/2 cup vegetable oil

1 cup all-purpose flour

1 teaspoon baking powder

1/2 cup sour cherry jam

9oz ricotta cheese

1/2 cup confectioners' sugar, for dusting

2/3 cup mixed berries (red currants, blackberries, rasperries, strawberries)

Preheat the oven to 350°F. Line a 14 x 8½-inch jelly roll pan or baking pan with a sheet of nonstick parchment paper.

Beat the eggs and extra yolk in a bowl together with the superfine sugar for 5 minutes until everything is light and fluffy. Gradually beat in the cocoa powder and vegetable oil before sifting in the flour and baking powder, beating all the while, to form a smooth batter.

Pour the batter into the prepared pan to form a thin layer, leveling it off with the back of a spoon. Bake for 15 minutes, or until lightly golden and springs back when lightly pressed with your fingertips. Remove the spongecake from the oven and let cool in the pan for a couple of minutes only (you want to be able to roll the cake while still hot so it doesn't break).

Once cooled slightly, remove the spongecake from the pan and spread the cherry jam evenly over its surface, then cover with the ricotta. With one of the shortest edges facing you, roll the spongecake up tightly into a log, using the parchment paper as a guide.

Dust the roll with confectioners' sugar and decorate with clusters of berries to serve.

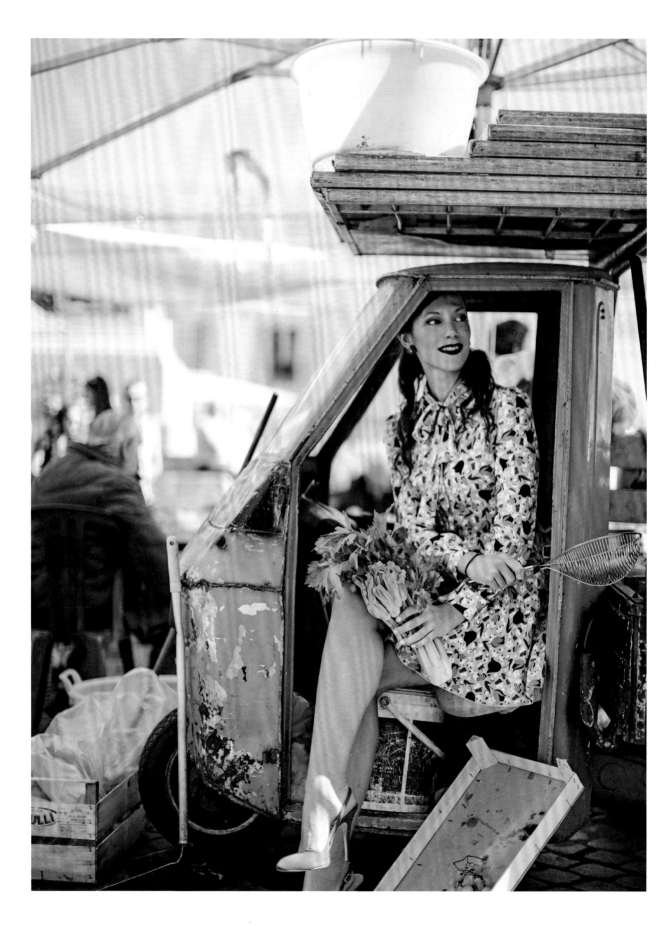

Chapter 10 PROVISIONS

Every September you'll hear inviting sizzling noises escaping from the kitchen windows of Rome. This time of year is all about stocking up the pantry for winter, and people will regularly share their handmade goodies. To me, this is yet further proof of how much cooking is an integral part of people's lives here—not just a hobby, but a highly valued form of communication. A handmade gift is the most genuine gesture.

When I enter Teresa's kitchen on Via del Pellegrino, she greets me with a kiss while handing me a bottle of *sugo* (*see* page 254). "You simply must have this sauce. Here!" she says, with ample gesticulation. Her kitchen, with its green Formica tables, is about to be filled with joy as she offers me some cheese accompanied by Red Onion Preserve (*see* page 263) and a few Breadsticks (*see* page 258). "At least you'll eat something, you're a bag of bones, sweetheart," she says, convinced that I'm somehow malnourished. Teresa, like many Roman women of her generation, loathes the young people's habit of consuming only three courses per meal. In her day, there would be an assortment of antipasti followed by *primi piatti* (pasta and rice), *secondi piatti* (meat and fish), *terzi piatti* (salad and cheese), *quarti piatti* (fruit), and *quinti piatti* (dessert). Twice a day, every day. And it is considered bad manners to leave even one piece of pasta on your plate. Never, ever.

There are still a few trattorias in Rome that perfectly correspond to my idea of off-the-beaten-track Roman food. Take, for example, Mami Trilussa, a temple of gluttony where you'll be served your carbonara directly in the pan, to make dunking the bread easier. For the best meat in town, I head to Cesare al Casaletto, a hidden gem just off the town's historical center. And when it comes to flawless tiramisù, I know that Settimio all'Arancio will never disappoint. Then, I'll stroll around the Roman triangle (Via Condotti, Via del Corso, Piazza di Spagna) and I know how I stand: still and in total veneration.

Restaurants in Rome—the trick lies in knowing where to find them. Go for a walk, don't let yourself be lured into a restaurant by a guy standing outside it calling out to you, and don't be afraid to enter the more modest ones: it's often in the less showy venues that you'll find tradition on display.

Carciofini sott'olio

ARTICHOKES IN OIL

I love the versatility of artichokes. Plenty of otherwise boring dishes acquire that much-needed extra depth of flavor thanks to their addition. There are hundreds of time-consuming ways to prepare these irresistible artichoke hearts, but why should it take a lifetime to make them when it only takes a couple of minutes to eat them? This recipe is a quick and easy compromise—another way of having your artichoke and eating it, too.

Preparation time: 5 minutes plus marinating

Makes 2 x 9-oz jars

1/4 cup lemon juice

1/2 cup extra virgin olive oil

1 teaspoon white wine vinegar

1 tablespoon salt

15 black peppercorns

1 teaspoon dried oregano

handful of mint leaves, chopped

9oz canned artichoke hearts in water, drained

Put the lemon juice, olive oil, vinegar, salt, peppercorns, oregano, and mint into a large food bag. Seal the bag securely and shake for 1 minute to mix everything together well.

Open the bag and add the artichoke hearts, then seal again and shake for 1 to 2 minutes, until the artichokes are evenly coated in oil.

Spoon the artichoke hearts into two sterilized jars (*see* page 254) and pour in the oil and vinegar mixture. Let the artichokes marinate for at least 2 hours before serving or store in a cool, dark place for up to 5 days.

Sugo passepartout per conserve, pizza e pasta

PASSEPARTOUT TOMATO SAUCE FOR PRESERVES, PIZZA & PASTA

Making your own tomato sauce is delightfully easy—the uncompromising honesty of the flavors will make you wonder why you waited so long to try it. I suggest you go for organic tomatoes ripened on the vine, if possible, though any vine tomato is fine.
Heat some oil in a pan, sweat some garlic and onion, and then add this juicy sauce. Let it reduce for about 20 minutes, stirring in a little boiling water halfway through, and that's it. The next time that need for a succulent tomato sauce arises, you'll open the jar, letting out all those Mediterranean flavors. Get ready to enter a new stage of kitchen intoxication.

Preparation time: 5 minutes

Cooking time: 6 minutes

Makes 2 x 1½-pint jars:

12 medium-sized firm vine-ripened tomatoes

2 tablespoons chopped basil, thyme, or rosemary leaves

salt

Start by sterilizing the jars. Preheat the oven to 250°F. Wash the jars and their lids in hot, soapy water, rinse thoroughly, and place in the oven for 10 minutes to dry completely.

Bring a large saucepan of salted water to a boil. Lower in the tomatoes and cook for 6 minutes or until the tomato skins just start to come away from the flesh. Remove the tomatoes with a slotted spoon, transfer to a food processor, and blend together with your chosen herb for 20 seconds or so to form a smooth sauce.

Spoon the sauce into the sterilized jars and screw the lids on firmly to close. Tie the jars together with a clean dish cloth (this will prevent them from moving around and getting chipped), put them into the saucepan upside down, and return the water to a boil. Boil for 30 minutes, then turn off the heat and let the jars cool in the pan for a further 30 minutes before removing from the water and drying.

Store the jars in a cool, dry place away from sunlight. The sauce will keep in the jars for up to 6 months.

Tozzetti della Tuscia con semi di chia

TUSCIAN TOZZETTI COOKIES WITH CHIA SEEDS

Sprawling is the archetypal after-lunch activity in Rome. After all, modern office life can prove hard, with the usual working day lasting between 4 and 6 hours, broken up by numerous modified coffee siestas, consisting of a shot of espresso with grappa, accompanied by a cookie and the latest gossip. I love to make these twice-baked crunchy cookies for special occasions. Dip them in any sweet wine you fancy—they'll make for a wonderful midday snack, waking you up from within. Better than delicious, they're Romanicious.

Preparation time: 15 minutes plus cooling

Cooking time: 35 minutes

Makes 30 cookies

1²/₃ cups whole almonds

4 eggs, plus 2 egg yolks, divided

1¹/₄ cups superfine sugar

pinch of salt

¹/₂ cup extra virgin olive oil

1 tablespoon sweet wine

1lb 6oz (5 cups) all-purpose flour, plus extra for dusting

2 teaspoons baking powder

2 tablespoons chia seeds

Heat the broiler to medium-high. Line two baking pans with parchment paper.

Spread the almonds in a single layer on one of the prepared baking pans and place under the broiler for 3 minutes until lightly golden. Transfer to a wire rack to cool.

Preheat the oven to 400°F.

Put the eggs, 1 egg yolk, sugar, and salt into the bowl of an electric stand mixer and beat together for 3 minutes until fluffy. Stir in the oil, wine, flour, and baking powder and continue to mix to form a smooth, slightly crumbly dough.

Add the almonds and chia seeds to the dough and fold together by hand, then divide the dough into 4 equal-sized pieces. On a clean, floured work surface, roll each dough piece out into a sausage-shaped log approximately 8 inches long. Transfer the dough logs to the prepared baking pan and brush with the remaining egg yolk. Bake for 20 minutes until pale gold in color, then remove from the oven and let cool for 30 minutes.

Once the dough logs have cooled, cut them into 1-inch pieces. Rearrange the cookies on the baking pan and bake for a further 10 minutes until firm and golden brown.

Let the cookies cool completely on a wire rack before serving. They can be kept, sealed in an airtight container, for up to 3 months.

Grissini

BREADSTICKS

Bread is one of the most heartening foods ever; I find it almost healing. So when I visit friends and find breadsticks on the table, I know that behind the scenes is a host with an eye for details. Whether I'm about to sit down to a lavish feast or a simple, everyday meal, I know I'm in for a treat.

For the breadsticks, measure the temperature of the water with a food thermometer, if possible, because you need to be quite precise. You can make the dough by hand, with a mixer, or in a bread machine. I prefer the latter, simply because I sometimes have an indolent nature.

Preparation time: 20 minutes plus rising

Cooking time: 15 minutes

Makes 30 breadsticks

1 cup bottled still or filtered water

$1^{1}/_{2}$ teaspoons fast-acting dry yeast

4 cups bread flour, divided

$^{1}/_{2}$ cup extra virgin olive oil

$2^{1}/_{2}$ teaspoons superfine sugar or
$1^{1}/_{2}$ teaspoons malt extract

1 tablespoon fine salt

$^{1}/_{3}$ cup sesame seeds or
poppy seeds

Pour the measured water into a pan. Using a food thermometer, check the temperature of the water—it should be 77°F—and gently heat it if necessary until it reaches the desired temperature. Pour the water into a large bowl along with the yeast and stir to dissolve. Add $^{3}/_{4}$ cup of the flour and stir everything together to form a wet dough. Let rest for 45 minutes.

Once rested, tip the yeast and flour mixture into the bowl of an electric stand mixer fitted the dough hook, add the oil, sugar, and remaining flour and knead together for 10 minutes to form a firm, elastic dough. Add the salt and knead for a further 3 minutes, then transfer the dough to a bowl, cover with plastic wrap, and let rise in a warm place for 1 hour, or until doubled in size.

Preheat the oven to 325°F.

Once risen, knock the dough back with your fists and shape it into a rectangle measuring $23^{1}/_{2}$ x 8 inches. Slice the dough lengthwise into strips $^{3}/_{4}$ inch in thickness using a sharp knife and roll each strip into a long, unevenly twisted cylinder. Place the breadsticks on a baking pan, spacing them about $^{1}/_{2}$ inch apart. Scatter with the sesame or poppy seeds and let rest for 15 minutes.

Bake the breadsticks in the oven for 15 minutes until golden brown (be sure to check them often to make sure they don't overcook). Transfer the breaadsticks to a wire rack to cool, then seal in an airtight container and store for up to 5 days.

Pangrattato

BREAD CRUMBS

I like to mix different odds and ends of bread in my bread crumbs, to make them more colorful and tasty.

Preparation time: 30 seconds

Makes 14oz

7oz stale bread

7oz stale breadsticks or crackers

1 teaspoon dried sage

Put all the ingredients in a food processor and blend together for 30 seconds or until they become fine bread crumbs. Store in an airtight container for up to 1 month.

Pesto Romano di zucchine

ROMAN-STYLE ZUCCHINI PESTO

I'm about to tackle a well-deserved glass of wine when my mother calls: she wants to know if I'm eating enough, sleeping enough, and why I have yet to turn into that perfect little girl. After one of these conversations I'm ravenous. Luckily, my freezer has treats in store for me. I like to spread this pesto on rye bread or dollop some on my *filetto* or pasta, and I'm in heaven.

Preparation time: 10 minutes plus draining

Makes 2 x 9-oz jars

2 zucchini

pinch of salt

2 teaspoons dried marjoram

1 garlic clove, peeled and left whole

15 basil leaves

2 tablespoons pine nuts

2 tablespoons extra virgin olive oil

1½oz pecorino romano cheese

1½oz Parmesan cheese

Start by sterilizing the jars (*see* page 254).

Slice the ends off the zucchini and discard. Cut the remainder into thin matchsticks. Put the zucchini pieces into a colander, place in the sink, and sprinkle with a pinch of salt. Let stand for 30 minutes to drain away any excess moisture.

Once drained, tip the zucchini pieces into a food processor with the marjoram, garlic, basil, pine nuts, oil, pecorino, and Parmesan and blend to a smooth, creamy paste. Spoon the pesto into the sterilized jam jars, seal with a lid, and refrigerate for up to 1 week, or transfer to a suitable container, seal, and freeze for up to 2 months.

Crostini

CROUTONS

Bread is sacred in Italy, and by that I mean you should never throw it away, since it could make a precious addition to numerous soups and salads. For this recipe, any stale bread will do.

Preparation time: 1 minute

Cooking time: 5 minutes

slices of stale bread

Cut the bread into ½-inch cubes and toast them in a nonstick skillet for about 5 minutes, stirring from time to time, until they are golden and browned at the edges.

Conserva alla cipolla rossa

RED ONION PRESERVE

Someone once told me a story set in Ancient Rome in which undiluted wine caught fire when it came too close to a lit candle. The wine back then was much higher in alcohol and couldn't possibly be drunk without being watered down first, though even today you can still find many people—especially those belonging to the older generation—pouring some water into their glass of red. I like to mix together my favorite leftover wine with sweet, burgundy-colored onions to make this preserve, the perfect accompaniment to a roast as well as all kinds of cheeses (see photograph overleaf). Be aware, though, that once you open the jar the onion preserve should be stored in the fridge and consumed within a week.

Preparation time: 5 minutes
plus macerating

Cooking time: 30 minutes

Makes 6 x 9-oz jars

3¼lb large red onions, peeled, halved, and thinly sliced

1 cup superfine sugar

1 cup light brown sugar, packed

⅔ cup rosé wine

3 tablespoons red wine vinegar

4 garlic cloves

2 kaffir lime leaves

Start by sterilizing the jars (*see* page 254).

Put all the ingredients into a large bowl. Stir well, cover with plastic wrap, and let macerate for at least 8 hours, preferably overnight.

When you're ready to cook, remove and discard the lime leaves from the softened onions and tip everything into a large Dutch oven. Bring to a gentle simmer and cook over low heat for 30 minutes, stirring occasionally, until the onions are soft and sticky and the mixture is thick and similar to jam in consistency.

To check that the preserve is ready, apply the following test: place a small saucer in the freezer for 10 minutes, then pour a few drops of the onion liquid onto the cold dish. After a minute, run your finger through the drops—if the preserve wrinkles slightly, it's good to go. If it doesn't, return the pan to the heat and simmer for a further 2 to 3 minutes, then retest.

Spoon the warm onion preserve into the sterilized jars, seal tightly, and store in a dry place away from sunlight for up to 6 months.

Marmellata di uva e noci pecan

GRAPE & PECAN JAM

The history of jam starts with melancholy. Catherine of Aragon, the unlucky first wife of Henry VIII, was said to have missed the fruits of her homeland so much that she had jams made and shipped to her from Spain to England.
Like the tan lines from your swimsuit, preserved fruit reminds us of carefree summer days as the autumn leaves start to fall. This grape and pecan jam makes a lovely change from the usual, and tastes wonderful spread on top of sweet melba toast (*see* page 35).

Preparation time: 20 minutes plus macerating

Cooking time: 1 hour

Makes 4 x 9-oz jars

2¼ lb red seedless grapes, halved

2 lemons, halved and thinly sliced

2½ cups superfine sugar

1 cup pecan nut halves

¼ cup brandy or cognac

Put the grape halves and lemon slices in a large bowl, add the sugar, and let macerate for 3 hours, until the juices start to run.

Remove the lemon slices from the bowl and discard. Then pour the rest of the mixture into a large saucepan. Bring to a simmer over low heat and cook for 1 hour, stirring frequently.

Meanwhile, sterilize the jars. Preheat the oven to 250°F. Wash the jars and their lids in hot, soapy water, rinse thoroughly, and place in the oven for 10 minutes to dry completely.

To check that the jam is ready, apply the following test: place a small plate in the freezer for 10 minutes, then pour a drop of jam onto the cold dish. Leave it for a minute, then flip the dish upside down—if the jam stays firmly attached to the dish and doesn't drop off, then it's good to go. If it does drop off, carry on simmering for 2 to 3 minutes, then retest.

Once ready, remove the jam from the heat and let cool for 5 minutes, then gently stir in the nuts and liqueur.

Pour the hot jam into the sterilized jars and screw the lids on firmly to seal. Turn the jars upside down to cool for 45 minutes, then flip them over. Store in the cupboard or pantry for up to 6 months.

Cubetti di ghiaccio

HANDMADE ICE CUBES

Gracefully clinking in glasses, ice cubes can be so much more than simply functional. To emphasize their power of suggestion and add a hint of color to my drinks, I like to enrich mine with all kinds of fruits, juices, and herbs. Are you planning to offer a fruity refreshment? Instead of water, just fill your ice cube trays with the fruit juice of your choice, put them into the freezer, and forget all about them until the next party. May the sun be with you.

Preparation time: 5 minutes plus freezing

Makes one regular ice-cube tray's worth

4 red grapes

$1/4$ kiwi, peeled

1 stalk red currants

8 mint leaves, halved

$2/3$ cup water or fresh fruit juice

Cut each grape in half and the kiwi into $1/8$-inch cubes. Strip the red currants from the stalk.

Fill half the molds of an ice-cube tray with the grape halves, kiwi pieces, and red currants, keeping the fruits separate. Top each mold with half a mint leaf and fill with water or juice. Freeze until solid (this will take at least 5 hours). These handmade ice cubes will keep in the freezer for up to 6 months.

Il Negroni

NEGRONI COCKTAIL

The Negroni can be "right" or "wrong." Either way, this bitter, candy-apple red aperitif is extremely soothing and relieves all kinds of post-work stress. The secret to its brilliant color? Cochineal, a scarlet dye now used primarily for coloring food that was once used by our grandmothers to dye wool or cotton.

The alternative version of this cocktail, the "wrong" one, is not wrong at all and is actually quite good. Known also as the *negroni sbagliato*, here prosecco is used instead of gin, making it much lighter. I like to add a hint of homemade Roman-style Sambuca (*see* page 271) and some Handmade Ice Cubes (*see* page 266) to make my Negronis. Fresh and vibrant, these cocktails are an impeccable way to get the party started. The recipe listed below calls for double servings and high spirits.

Preparation time: 5 minutes plus chilling

Serves 4

4 Handmade Ice Cubes (*see* page 266) or regular ice cubes, crushed

8½fl oz gin or prosecco

8½fl oz red vermouth

8½fl oz Campari or Gran Classico

4 dashes of Roman-style Sambuca (*see* page 271) or regular sambuca

4 orange twists, to garnish

Place 4 martini glasses in the freezer to chill for 10 minutes.

Line up the chilled glasses on a work surface and add crushed ice to each. Pour one-quarter of the gin or prosecco, vermouth, and Campari or Gran Classico into each glass and finish with a dash of sambuca. Stir together, garnish with the orange twists, and serve.

Sambuca alla Romana

ROMAN-STYLE SAMBUCA

Some types of cooking are therapeutic, time spent in joyful activity. Other culinary processes, such as the one involved in making a liqueur, for example, resemble a propitiatory ritual. Here night-sky dark star anise, bronze cinnamon, and a hint of coriander make up the ingredients of this famous liqueur, which is also used in the making of Tarallucci al Vino (*see* page 43). Sooner or later, everyone in Rome drinks it, often dropping a couple of roasted coffee beans in the glass for extra aroma. After all that food, you need a little bitterness to prepare you for the next banquet. And leave you happily oblivious, of course.

Preparation time: 10 minutes plus 23 days storing

Makes 2 x 1-quart bottles

3oz star anise

1 teaspoon coriander seeds

1 cinnamon stick

4 cloves

1 vanilla bean

1 lemon

24fl oz eau-de-vie (colorless fruit liqueur), 40 to 80% proof

2½ cups superfine sugar

4 cups water

Place the star anise, coriander seeds, cinnamon stick, cloves, vanilla bean, and lemon in a 2-quart Kilner jar, pour in the eau-de-vie, and seal tightly. Store for 20 days in a dark, dry place, giving the jar a shake every other day to allow all the ingredients to mingle.

After the 20 days are up, dissolve the sugar in the measured water and add to the jar. Close the jar and let stand for a further 3 days, then strain the liqueur into two clean, dry bottles. Enjoy immediately or store for up to 2 years.

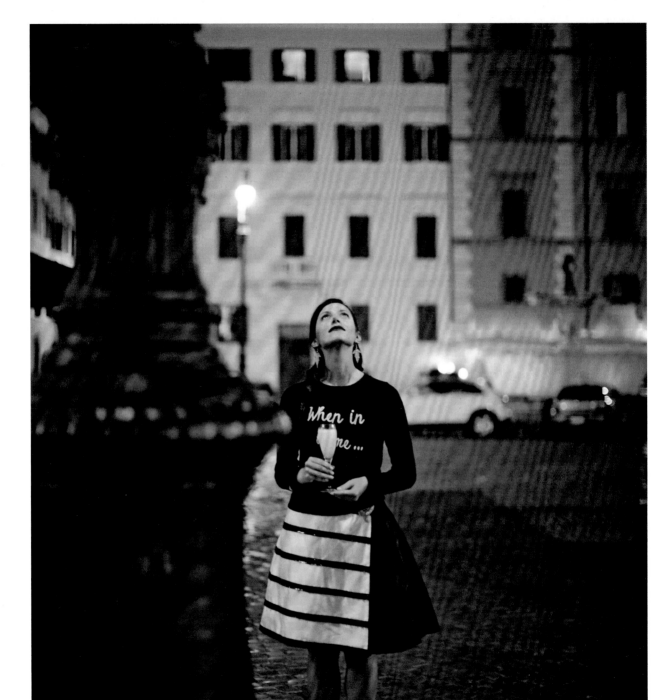

Chapter II
MIDNIGHT MUNCHIES

These days, Via dei Coronari, the road of the crown makers, is home to the most exclusive antique shops and jewelers. Not far from here, you will find La Casa di Fiammetta, once the home of Cesare Borgia's mistress. Right around the corner, Via del Governo Vecchio is the road of the old government. Once dominated by the unrivaled supremacy of the Pope, the street now boasts an undisputedly great *osteria*, Da Tonino, serving *straccetti* (*see* page 279) and *fusilli aglio e olio* (*see* page 290). Pontiffs have traveled the length of Via del Governo Vecchio for centuries, sitting on a ceremonial throne carried on the shoulders of the offspring of Rome's A-listers, next in line for power. These young men would often crack jokes at the expense of their passenger, who would amiably punish them by sending them to the fortified Castel Sant'Angelo, the papal jail, for a few days of isolated contemplation with room service.

Somewhere on this awfully charming road, you might bump into Dolores. This local legend—her green eyes glowing like a Sgroppino (*see* page 295) as she tells you about her adventures working as an extra for Federico Fellini—now sleeps under the stars. Some say she once possessed a fortune in precious jewels and other gifts from her lovers, others talk about her addiction to lust and Affogato al Caffè (*see* page 293). Did she ever really work with the director of *La Dolce Vita*? Despite her bruised appearance today, you might still find a glance of past glory in her sneaky smile . . . maybe.

The first "talking statue" of Rome, Pasquino gave voice to those who would find it too transgressive or hazardous to share their discontent with state or church in public, in the days before freedom of speech for all. Women and men of all kinds came to the ruined Greek statue on the corner of Piazza Pasquino, their heads covered by black veils. Complaints and protests would appear on the statue in the form of satirical poems, styled with wit, subtlety, and a huge amount of derision. Public figures were caricatured in words: some were transformed into monuments, some into animals, some even into Carciofi alla Romana (see *page* 283). Dishes of Rome styled up for all kitchens.

Grattachecca

ROMAN GRANITA

To me, there's nothing more emblematic of the torrid Roman summer than this ice-cold dessert: it's only when the *grattachecca* kiosks open again that I know the time of eternal flirtation and sunburn has arrived. A day trip to the coastal town of Sperlonga, home of the grotto of Tiberius and some seriously amazing mozzarella, wouldn't be the same if it didn't end, after the inevitable traffic jam on the way back to Rome, with a visit to Alla Fonte d'Oro, the oldest *grattacheccaro* in Trastevere. There are two occasions on which I like to consume this granita: when it's so hot that your internal thermometer is rendered useless, and when spring is in full blossom, allowing you to regain your grasp on the flavors of the warmer seasons, lost during the winter. Here is an easy, do-it-yourself version.

Preparation time: 5 minutes plus cooling

Cooking time: 5 minutes

Serves 4

1²/₃ cups strawberries, hulled and halved, or other berries

2 tablespoons lemon juice

¹/₂ cup confectioners' sugar

30 ice cubes

¹/₄ cup coconut chunks, banana slices, or other fruit pieces, to decorate

small handful of mint leaves

Gently heat the strawberries in a small nonstick skillet for 3 minutes until they have softened and collapsed. Using a potato masher, crush the strawberries into a thick paste. Whisk in the lemon juice and sugar and simmer for a further 3 minutes until everything has reduced down to a syrup. Sieve the syrup into a bowl and transfer to the refrigerator. Let cool for 1 hour.

When ready to serve, take the ice out of the freezer, place it in a large freezer bag, and seal it securely. Using a rolling pin or ice crusher, if you have one, smash the ice to a slushy consistency.

Divide the crushed ice between 4 glass dessert dishes or glasses. Pour in the fruit syrup and stir together with a cocktail spoon. Decorate with coconut chunks, banana slices, or fruit chunks of your choice, and finish with a few mint leaves.

Pallotte cacio e ova

SHALLOW-FRIED CHEESE & EGG BALLS

This is a dish made from simple ingredients, found in all Roman homes, but I think this general rule can also be extended in some form to this book's lovely readers—I assume we all have some leftover soft cheese in the fridge, waiting to be put to good use. There's something unmistakably honest about eating leftovers, maybe because the cook's good intentions have been applied to the ingredients for a second time, and most eloquently, too. The added egg helps bind together all the other ingredients, as it does in so many recipes. These balls don't take long to prepare. Once they've browned in the hot oil, they can be considered done.

Preparation time: 10 minutes

Cooking time: 20 minutes

Makes 20 *pallotte*

1/2 cup milk

5 1/2 oz stale bread, torn into small pieces

9oz ricotta, cottage cheese, or other mild, soft cheese

1 large egg

handful of flat-leaf parsley leaves, chopped

2 teaspoons salt

2 garlic cloves, thinly sliced, divided

1/2 cup vegetable or olive oil, divided

1 x 9-oz can cherry tomatoes

1/4 teaspoon superfine sugar

handful of basil leaves, chopped, plus extra whole leaves, to garnish

1 teaspoon pink peppercorns

Pour the milk into a small bowl, add the bread pieces, and let soak briefly.

Squeeze any excess milk out of the bread, then tip it into a bowl with the cheese, egg, parsley, salt, and half the sliced garlic. Using your hands, mix everything together well, then roll the mixture into walnut-sized balls.

Heat 2 tablespoons of oil in a skillet, add the tomatoes, sugar, chopped basil, and remaining garlic. Season with salt, bring to a simmer, and cook for 10 minutes until the sauce has thickened and reduced slightly.

Meanwhile, heat the remaining vegetable oil in a large nonstick skillet over medium heat until hot. Carefully lower the cheese and egg balls into the oil and fry for 5 minutes until golden brown. Lift the balls out of the skillet using a slotted spoon and place them on a dish covered with paper towels to drain off any excess oil.

Carefully add the fried balls to the sauce and cook for a further 2 to 3 minutes to warm through, then transfer to a serving platter. Scatter with the pink peppercorns and a few whole basil leaves to garnish, and serve.

Straccetti al Marsala accompagnati da spinaci e pane raffermo

SLICED VEAL WITH MARSALA ACCOMPANIED BY SPINACH & STALE BREAD

A paparazzo is a photographer whose job it is to capture the rich and famous in the most compromising situations. The word was used for the first time in Fellini's *La Dolce Vita*, for a slimy and persistent character who strolls around Rome eager to take unofficial pictures in order to gain fame or (better still) infamy. Many celebrities have fought the invasive nature of the paparazzi with explosive public outbursts, while some have made the photographers promise to tear their worst pictures into strips.
The original version of this dish calls for beef, but you can use any kind of meat. Just reduce it to strips and you'll have your *straccetti* all worked out. As simple as taking a picture.

Preparation time: 10 minutes

Cooking time: 20 minutes

Serves 6

2/3 cup all-purpose flour

1 teaspoon ground turmeric

1lb 5oz organic veal or pork
    scallops, cut into 1/2-inch slices

3 tablespoons extra virgin olive oil

walnut-sized lump of unsalted
    butter

1/3 cup Marsala wine

a drop of soy sauce

2 tablespoons cornstarch mixed
    together with 1/2 cup water

Spinach:

1lb 2oz spinach leaves

51/2oz stale bread, cut into
    1/2-inch cubes

3oz pancetta cubes

1 garlic clove, peeled and left whole

2 tablespoons extra virgin olive oil

2 tablespoons grated pecorino
    romano cheese

salt

Place the flour and turmeric in a plastic food bag, add the veal slices, seal the bag securely, and shake to coat.

Heat the oil and butter together in a large skillet over medium heat. Add the coated meat pieces and cook, stirring occasionally, for 5 minutes until lightly golden on each side. Remove the meat from the pan and set aside.

Pour the Marsala, soy sauce, and cornstarch solution into the pan, bring to a simmer, and let the mixture bubble away for 5 minutes until thickened and reduced.

While the sauce is reducing, cook the spinach. Put the spinach leaves in a large saucepan and add just enough boiling water to cover. Season with salt, bring to a simmer, and cook over medium heat for 5 minutes, then add the bread and stir everything together well to allow it to soak up the cooking liquid. Tip the mixture into a colander to drain off any excess liquid, then return it to the pan and mash everything together coarsely with a fork or potato masher.

Heat a small nonstick skillet over low heat, add the pancetta, and fry for 2 to 3 minutes, until the pancetta has rendered some of its fat. Add the garlic and cook for a further 3 minutes until the pancetta is crisp and golden, then tip the garlic and pancetta into the mashed spinach and mix together well. Stir in the olive oil and season with salt to taste.

Return the veal pieces to the sauce and warm through for 1 to 2 minutes, then divide between plates. Sprinkle the spinach with the grated pecorino and serve.

ROMAN STYLE BRAISED ARTICHOKES

Behind the Circus Maximus, among the marvels of the Palatine ruins, there's a rose garden comprising more than 1,100 rose varieties. I'm surprised that no artichokes grow here, because to me this is the vegetable most reminiscent of the most romantic flower of them all. Not only is it fragrantly delicious at first bite, its aftertaste is just heavenly. When artichokes are in season, Romans eat them like a panacea for all life's worries. The good news is that they are low in calories and make a terrific liver cleanser. Hearty and fulfilling. Rejoice. These artichokes will keep in the refrigerator for up to five days and are excellent added to pasta or served alongside poached eggs.

Preparation time: 15 minutes

Cooking time: 40 minutes

Serves 4

large handful of mint leaves, divided

2 kaffir lime leaves, finely chopped

1 garlic clove, minced

1 cup bread crumbs (*see* page 262)

3 tablespoons extra virgin olive oil

4 long-stemmed artichokes, cleaned (*see* page 13) and placed in acidulated water

2/3 cup vegetable stock

salt

Finely chop half the mint and put it in a bowl with the lime leaves, garlic, bread crumbs, and 1 tablespoon of the extra virgin olive oil. Season with salt and mix together well.

Delicately pry open the cavity of each prepared artichoke with a teaspoon and fill with 4 teaspoons of the herb mixture.

Gently heat the remaining 2 tablespoons of olive oil in a large saucepan over very low heat. Add the artichokes to the pan stem-side up and pour the vegetable stock over them.

Scatter with the remaining mint leaves, bring to a simmer, and cook over medium–low heat, covered, for 40 minutes, until the thickest part of the artichoke stem is tender to the point of a sharp knife.

Season the artichokes with salt to taste and transfer to a serving dish. Serve hot or, for best results, let cool to room temperature before serving.

Salsiccia con lenticchie, porro e finocchio

BRAISED SAUSAGES WITH LENTILS, LEEKS & FENNEL

I can't get enough of these nutty legumes, which are considered a symbol of good luck in Italy and are so easily matched with a large range of ingredients. They make a wonderful addition to stews, soups, and salads, and they're also a great meat substitute. There's a salami in Italy called *finocchiona*—it's one of those foods that lift you up no matter what life throws at you. It's more of a countryside delicacy, not available all year round or easy to find, but I like to recreate its smells and flavors in my own kitchen with this one-pot supper, to be devored on the couch in front of your favorite old movie.

Preparation time: 5 minutes

Cooking time: 30 minutes

Serves 4

¼ cup extra virgin olive oil

1 leek, trimmed, cleaned, and finely sliced lengthwise

1 fennel bulb, trimmed and cut into coarse strips

14oz pork sausages

1¼ cups Castelluccio or Puy lentils

1½ cups vegetable stock

1½ tablespoons fennel seeds

small handful of chives, snipped

salt and pepper

Warm the oil in a skillet over medium heat, add the leek, and fry for 5 minutes until softened and translucent. Add the fennel and sausages and cook for a further 5 minutes until the sausages are browned on all sides.

Add the lentils to the pan and pour in the stock. Bring to a boil, then reduce the heat to a gentle simmer and let cook for 25 minutes, or until the lentils have softened and the sausages are cooked through. Season with salt and pepper to taste.

Divide the lentils and sausages between plates. Scatter them with the fennel seeds and chopped chives to finish, and serve.

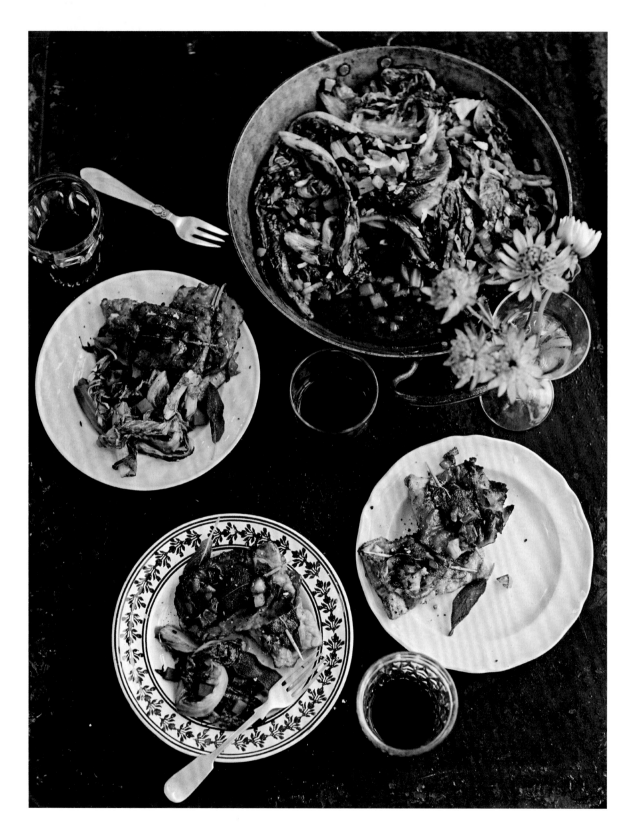

Saltimbocca alla Romana con pera caramellata, salvia fritta e lattuga brasata

ROMAN-STYLE SALTIMBOCCA WITH CARAMELIZED PEAR, FRIED SAGE & BRAISED LETTUCE

Preparation time: 25 minutes

Cooking time: 40 minutes

Serves 4

1 stick unsalted butter, divided

1 tablespoon superfine sugar

10 sage leaves, 2 finely chopped and 8 left whole

½ pear, peeled, cored, and cut into small chunks

8 x 2½-oz organic veal scallops, trimmed

¼ cup all-purpose flour

4 x ¼-oz prosciutto slices, halved

⅔ cup white wine

Braised lettuce:

1lb 2oz lettuce, trimmed and leaves separated

1 carrot, cut into ½-inch cubes

1 large white onion, cut into ½-inch cubes

3 tablespoons extra virgin olive oil

1 teaspoon chopped thyme leaves

1 teaspoon chopped tarragon leaves

1 teaspoon chopped flat-leaf parsley leaves

1 cup vegetable stock

Fried sage:

1 tablespoon all-purpose flour

3 tablespoons sparkling water

3 tablespoons extra virgin olive oil

3 salted anchovies, rinsed and cut into ½-inch pieces

25 sage leaves

As challenging or cheerful as my day may have been, when nighttime comes, wherever in the world I might be, I make my way to the kitchen. This way, I'll always be at home. For this recipe, you'll need to pound the meat for it to really melt in the mouth. If you don't have a meat mallet, take a heavy skillet, cover your meat with plastic wrap, and bash away. It's also a great way to relieve the stress of a working day.

Preheat the oven to 400°F.

For the braised lettuce, bring a large saucepan of salted water to a boil, add the lettuce leaves, and blanch for 3 minutes. Drain the lettuce well and rinse under cold running water, then put into a baking dish along with the carrot and onion pieces. Drizzle with the oil, scatter with the chopped herbs, and mix together well. Then pour in the stock, cover with parchment paper, and cook in the oven for 30 minutes, or until all the stock has been absorbed and the vegetables are soft and tender.

While the lettuce is cooking, prepare the *saltimbocca*. Melt half the butter in a small saucepan over low heat. Add the sugar, chopped sage leaves, and pear to the pan and cook for 10 minutes, or until the pear chunks are tender but still holding their shape. Remove from the heat and set aside.

Bash the veal pieces out as thinly and evenly as possible (see above), then dust with the flour, shaking off the excess. Spoon a teaspoon of the pear mixture into the center of a veal piece and press a piece of prosciutto on top to create a parcel. Top the prosciutto with a sage leaf and skewer with a toothpick to fix everything in place. Repeat with the remaining ingredients.

Gently heat the remaining butter in a large skillet. Add the veal, prosciutto-side down, and cook for 2 minutes on each side, turning carefully, until golden (you may need to do this in batches). Remove the veal scallops and transfer to a low oven (300 to 325°F) to keep warm. Add the white wine to the pan and bring to a boil over high heat. Season with salt and pepper and reduce until syrupy.

For the fried sage, mix together the flour, water, and a pinch of salt to form a batter. Heat the olive oil in a skillet. Sandwich the anchovy pieces between the sage leaves, dip them in the batter, and fry for about 1 minute per side, until golden brown. Drain the crispy sage leaves on paper towels and scatter them over the saltimbocca. Serve with the braised lettuce.

Pappa al pomodoro

BREAD & TOMATO SOUP

"Viva la Pappa col Pomodoro" is a popular tune sung by Rita Pavone, a teen star back in the Sixties. As well as singing about this dish, she also played the title character in one of Italy's first ever TV series, *Il Giornalino di Gian Burrasca*—a boy whose name translates as "Johnny Tempest." This nickname, which the boy was given by his family because of his bad behavior (more a matter of exuberance than malice), has since become proverbial, and is now given to any unruly kid. Bread and tomato, the quintessential Italian combination that never goes wrong, even if all else does.

Preparation time: 20 minutes

Cooking time: 25 minutes

Serves 4

3 tablespoons extra virgin olive oil, divided

1 scallion, finely chopped

2¾ cups cherry tomatoes, halved

large handful of basil leaves, coarsely chopped

1 teaspoon ground nutmeg

½ cup vegetable stock

1 round crusty sourdough loaf or 4 crusty bread rolls

1 garlic clove, peeled and cut in half

pinch of red chili flakes

zest of 1 lemon

basil leaves, to garnish

salt

Gently heat 2 tablespoons of olive oil in a skillet, add the scallion, and let cook over low heat, stirring occasionally, for 5 minutes until softened and lightly golden.

Add the tomatoes, chopped basil, and nutmeg and cook, stirring, for 10 minutes. Pour in the stock, bring to a gentle simmer, and cook for a further 10 minutes until everything has reduced to a thick sauce.

Cut the top off of the loaf of bread or of each bread roll , if using, and carefully scoop out the insides to form a bread "bowl," being careful to keep the crust intact. Rub the removed bread with the garlic halves, tear it into thumb-sized pieces, and toast it for 3 minutes in a dry skillet over medium heat.

Tip the toasted bread pieces into the tomato sauce and season with salt. Sprinkle with the red chili flakes, then stir everything together until thick and silky in texture. Remove from the heat, drizzle with the remaining tablespoon of olive oil, and spoon the soup into the loaf or bread rolls. Scatter with the lemon zest and some basil leaves to serve.

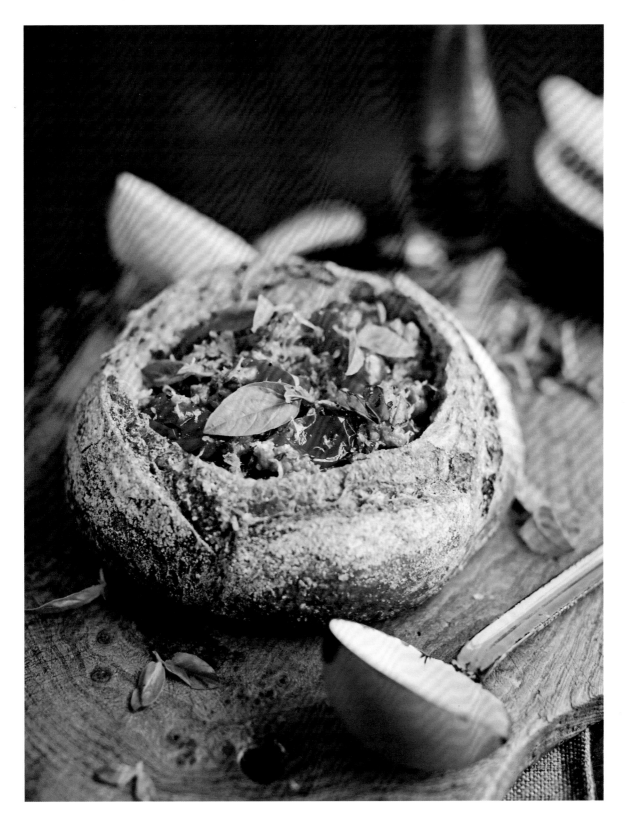

Fusilli lunghi aglio, olio, indivia, peperoncino, capperi e molliche

FUSILLI PASTA WITH GARLIC, OLIVE OIL, ENDIVE, CHILIES, CAPERS & BREADCRUMBS

This plain and extremely simple Roman dish is one of the first things Italian kids attempt to cook. The name of the recipe itself echoes with the far-from-perfect Roman dialect: *"aio, oio e peperoncino,"* which is how we are all used to hearing it pronounced. I like to give this dish a Roman look with a little of my own style, of course. *Colatura di alici* is the amber-colored, aromatic juice of salted anchovies. It can be difficult to find, so to replace it, I cook some anchovies in the most exquisite extra virgin olive oil I can find. A long spiral-shaped type of pasta like fusilli lunghi is perfect for this sauce, but any long pasta shape will do.

Preparation time: 10 minutes

Cooking time: 10 minutes

Serves 4

12oz fusilli lunghi or linguine pasta

1/2 cup extra virgin olive oil

2 garlic cloves, peeled and left whole

4 anchovies in olive oil

2 Belgian endives, trimmed and finely sliced

1 teaspoon chopped fresh red chili or dried red chili flakes

1 teaspoon salted capers, rinsed

large handful of flat-leaf parsley leaves, finely chopped, plus extra to garnish

1 1/2 tablespoons unsalted butter

1 3/4oz stale bread, cut into 1/2-inch cubes, to garnish

salt

Bring a large saucepan of salted water to a boil. Add the pasta and cook following the package directions until *al dente.*

While the pasta is cooking, prepare the sauce. Gently heat the olive oil in a large nonstick skillet with the garlic and anchovies, stirring occasionally, until the anchovies have dissolved. Stir in the endives, fresh or dried chili, and capers.

Once cooked, drain the pasta, reserving a ladleful of the cooking water. Tip the pasta into the sauce, add the parsley, butter, and pasta cooking water and stir everything together well.

To serve, divide the pasta between bowls and scatter with the bread cubes (which you could quickly toast in a nonstick skillet first, for extra crunchiness) and scatter with a little extra chopped parsley to garnish.

ICE-CREAM DROWNED IN COFFEE

This traditional recipe, typical of the Italian summer, combines two classics of Italian gastronomy—artisanal gelato and coffee. In Italy we all make coffee with a moka pot, but other methods are fine: it's a dense and bitter espresso-type coffee you're after. Below I'm offering you a recipe for fuss-free homemade gelato, but if you want to go for ready-made ice cream, the flavors that are best suited to being drowned in coffee are vanilla, *stracciatella*, and the nutty ones, like praline. Fruity flavors don't work well with coffee so avoid them. Remember, the scoop of gelato for each serving needs to be appropriately indulgent.

Preparation time: 10 minutes plus freezing

Cooking time: 5 minutes

Serves 4

4 shots hot good-quality espresso coffee

4 teaspoons superfine sugar

1/2 cup unsalted pistachios, crushed

Homemade gelato:

1 1/2 cups milk

1/4 cup superfine sugar

3/4 cup hazelnuts

For the homemade gelato, pour the milk into an ice-cube tray, place in the freezer, and let freeze until solid (this will take at least 5 hours).

When the frozen milk is ready, make the espressos and sweeten them with the sugar while still hot. Set aside to cool for 10 minutes.

In a food processor, mix the sugar and hazelnuts together to a fine powder. Add the frozen milk and blend together for a few seconds until you get an ice-cream consistency. The time this takes varies depending on the machine you're using, so watch it closely.

Scoop the ice cream into 4 glass dessert dishes and pour the coffee around each (if you pour the coffee directly on top, the ice cream will melt and it will spoil the presentation). Sprinkle with the crushed pistachios and enjoy immediately.

Sgroppino

FROTHY LEMON SORBET

In Italy, when people talk about finishing a lavish meal, you will often hear comments like: "We had fruit, dessert, coffee, and coffee killers." Coffee killers often come in the form of dessert wines or liqueurs and this is the category you would also put *sgroppino* in, though it has a lighter feel to it and a lower alcohol content than most. If you have never tasted this citrusy delicacy before, then I strongly suggest you do so. And if you have, forget about all the rules and follow this ridiculously easy recipe for a glorious end to a meal. I like to serve this sorbet in vintage champagne glasses. Also, I would recommend that you have a little extra on hand, because this surely calls for seconds and thirds and . . .

Preparation time: 5 minutes

Serves 4

½ cup lemon ice cream

approximately 1¾ cups prosecco

2 teaspoons ground nutmeg

1 teaspoon freshly ground black pepper

zest of 1 lemon, to garnish

Place the ice cream in a large bowl and beat it with a balloon whisk for 1 to 2 minutes to soften it up slightly. Gradually add the prosecco, continuing to whisk, until the mixture is light, creamy, and fluffy in consistency, then whisk in the nutmeg and pepper. Pour the *sgroppino* into champagne glasses, and sprinkle with the lemon zest to garnish. Enjoy immediately.

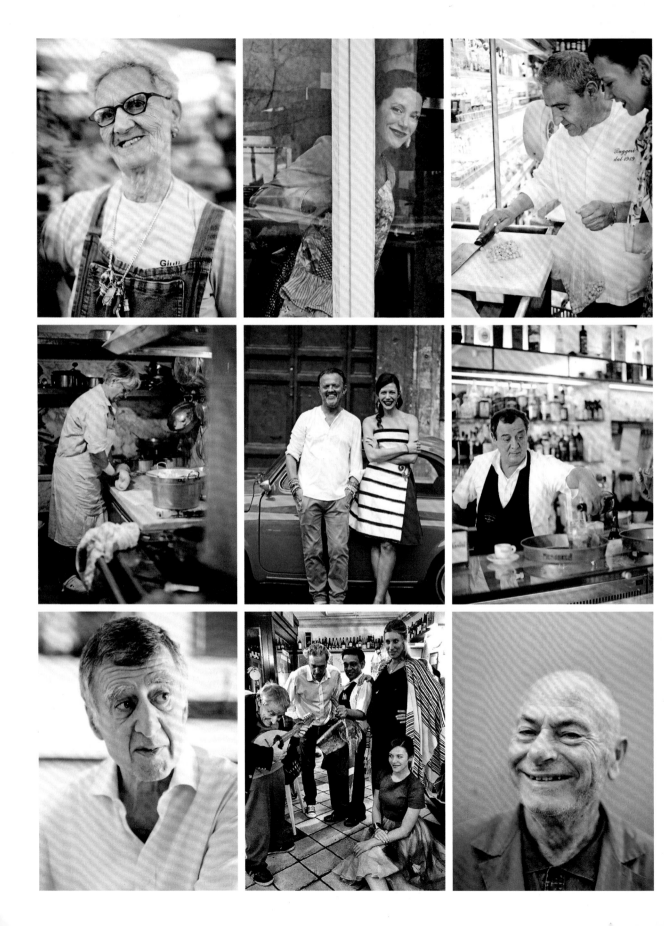

Ringraziamenti

ACKNOWLEDGMENTS

I've spent the most incredible year making this book, which gorgeously enriched my life. I'm absolutely thrilled and overwhelmed with joy to be surrounded by a remarkable group of people who have provided an unbreakable chain of support that is nothing short of spectacular. Therefore my thanks go first and foremost to the extraordinary Octopus Publishing Group for the contagious enthusiasm of making my Roman gastronomic adventures an attainable achievement since day one. Among them:

My commissioning editor, Eleanor Maxfield, for confidently hiring me as a first-time author and allowing me to write this book, thus including me in the fine presence of the company's great authors, who have entertained and influenced me for so many years before this book even came to life. It feels such a triumph for me to be on this list.

The fantastic Alex Stetter for editing my book and giving me the chance to own my voice throughout the pages and supporting my vision all along. Thank you for sharing this journey with me.

Art Director Juliette Norsworthy. It was a privilege to get through the graphic and creative process with you. Thank you for your dedication and commitment.

Natalie Bradley, for always making sure I'm on time.

Caroline Alberti, for making this book look beautiful.

Caroline Brown, Kevin Hawkins, and the sublime Publicity and Sales departments for so bravely and intelligently showing me the way in this tremendous industry and being so eternally optimistic.

Everything I've shown through this book I got by picking up that phone, talking about my ideas, and being given a chance by my brilliant agent Federica Leonardis at Rogers, Coleridge and White. That changed my life. You're largely responsible for this *opera prima*; this would not have happened without you. Thank you for fearlessly stepping into this adventure and trusting and supporting me by way of sheer enlightenment, and for not putting a restraining order on my emails, even when you're on vacation.

The photography maestro David Loftus, who worked so hard to keep me safe and make me laugh, without whose incredible professionalism, talent and humanity this book wouldn't be the treasure it is. These pictures were sinfully fun to make and I hope it shows. Thank you for flawlessly adapting your images to my words.

The sweet and hugely gifted food and prop stylists Emily Ezekiel and Linda Berlin, for all their hard work during the photoshoot days. Thank you for embodying my faith in timeless women, those with a capital W, who should never take the back seat.

The designers at Fendi, Red Valentino, Renato Balestra, and Beulah, who let me rove their closets and look pretty in their dresses to beautifully convey that *Dolce Vita* style. Sorry if I broke a few heels on *sanpietrini* (cobblestones) in the process.

La Belle Assiette for letting me bring my #foodhappiness into people's homes.

All my friends who've tested my recipes, for being so receptive and wild and funny and, much to my astonishment, happy at the outcome—particularly Ginevra Boralevi, Rodolphe & Maggie Frerejean Taittinger, Matteo Basilé & Teresa Emanuele, Francesco Ruspoli & Angelica Visconti, Arnaud de Giovanni, Anne Helia Roure, Helene Bernowitz.

Ringraziamenti
ACKNOWLEDGMENTS

Giovanna Rispoli for having so generously hosted me at your Capri retreat, and for the calm, cool, sun-breezed days during which to work without interruption.

Anna & Sergio Gelmi di Caporiacco, for taking such good care of me during my writing process and beyond, providing me with a peaceful cocoon in which to write, a kitchen in which to test my recipes, and warm hospitality. I'm eternally grateful for your unparalleled sense of family and patience.

Artico, you rock my life. Thank you for keeping me on track, thank God for your stubbornness, thank God for everything about you: all I value in life, you've given me. You truly made me want to be the best woman I supposed I never knew I could be.

I wouldn't have written this book had I not understood love and its tremendous magnitude, and for that I thank my beloved and glorious great-grandmother Nonna Ia, who was the most beautiful and brave woman I've ever known, encompassing all qualities a human being should be provided with. Thank you for your undivided love and generosity, and for showing me by example what endearing power it is to share life with and for others.

My dear brother Giuseppe, thanks for continuing to push the boundaries of what's possible. You are my earthly guardian angel whose wisdom and guidance I have always looked up to.

Profound thanks to the incandescent Instagram community for all the tips and the constant support.

I am grateful for being allowed to use the wonderful locations at Antico Caffè Greco, Trattoria Settimio al Pellegrino, Bar del Fico, Bar Perù, and the farmers' markets on Via della Croce and Piazza Campo dei Fiori.

Last but not least, thank you to the heroism and courage of the butcher, the shoemaker, the artisans, the market traders—they represent a world of unmatched excellence. Their portrayal not only shines a light on those artisanal jobs that are too often left out, but it shows Rome and their passion, their vulnerability, their humor, and their extraordinary depth, which are far too exceptional to be ignored. #foodhappiness and Roman tradition need to be upheld.

Eleonora Galasso is a food writer, blogger, teacher, and Instagram sensation. Her love of food began at an early age: she was forbidden from entering her great-grandmother's kitchen, but she was allowed to taste the pasta to make sure it was *al dente*. As is often the case in life, an obstacle turned a girl's curiosity into a hobby and a career. She went on to train at the Ateneo Italiano della Cucina in Rome before completing a Master's degree in gastronomy and food culture. For her first cookbook, Eleonora traveled the Lazio region extensively, accumulating recipes and stories from an eclectic cast of characters and bringing them to life with her unique creative touch.

Today Eleonora zigzags between Rome and Paris, working as a journalist and running cooking workshops, as well as collaborating with major international food brands and companies.